In Praise of *De*

"*Dear Diary Boy* is a **heart-wrenching, revelatory and shocking memoir** that opens a fascinating window into the world of traditional Japanese education. Kumiko Makihara tells **a beautiful and universal story of the hard choices so many women face and the depth of a mother's love.**"

—Amy Chua, Yale Law professor and author
   of *Battle Hymn of the Tiger Mother* and
   Political Tribes

"Kumiko Makihara has written **a spare, thoughtful gem of a book** about the education of her charming if exasperating son that should be read by anyone interested in modern Japan. It speaks volumes about motherhood, boyhood, cross-cultural adjustment and the power of conformism and parental ambition everywhere."

—Jonathan Alter, author of *The Center Holds: Obama and His Enemies*

"To straddle two cultures is to feel always, to some extent, a stranger; add in the strange country of motherhood, and things become even more difficult. Kumiko Makihara's memoir—**anguished, defiant, joyful, and unflinchingly honest**—is difficult to read but harder to put down. In our increasingly hybrid global culture, **it is an important story.**"

—Janice P. Nimura, author of *Daughters of the Samurai: A Journey from East to West and Back*

"A compulsively readable memoir that is at once horrifying and hysterical. This cautionary tale reveals volumes about Japan and about mothering."

—**Barbara Demick, author of *Nothing to Envy***

"Kumiko Makihara's **eloquent memoir offers a rare glimpse into Japanese parenting from deep inside.** She is a conscientious mother jumping to meet the challenges thrown her way by an elite Tokyo school, but the struggles are daunting, as she and her son search for their own place in the system. **At once moving, distressing, hilarious and very informative.**"

—**Stacy Perman, author of *In-N-Out Burger* and *A Grand Complication***

"**Hilarious and poignant.** Any parent swept up in our testing culture will understand how Kumiko Makihara's hopes and dreams gave way to the insanity of competition in a Japanese elementary school. And they will marvel at Taro's refreshing oblivion to the crazy culture in which he is immersed."

—**Debbie Stier, author of *The Perfect Score Project***

"**Compulsively readable, hilarious and hopeful,** Kumiko Makihara's memoir tells two stories—one of a mother and son traversing the treacherous 21st century terrain of private education—the other of a sensitive writer whose own creative spark was nearly extinguished by culture, society, gender and her own well-meaning parents. With writing that is lyrical and emotional but without an ounce of sentimentality, she captures the fleeting wonder of childhood and the particular pain of a parent tasked with ushering that spirit into the realities of adulthood. **A must-read for any parent who's ever wondered when to step in and when to step back.**"

— Kathryn Bowers, author of *Zoobiquity* and *Wildhood*

"*Dear Diary Boy* is **a poignant story of the lengths a mother will go for her son. It's also an insightful portrayal of the conformity of Japanese society.** Anyone who has ever felt like an outsider will relate to Kumiko Makihara's book."

— Elliott Holt, author of *You Are One of Them*

"*Dear Diary Boy* is a wrenching, deeply personal and compulsively readable love letter from a single mother to her adopted son. Makihara swings between anger, love, guilt, remorse and occasionally desperation as she tries to plot a path for her son through Japan's familial and schooling strictures. **The book is both a cross-cultural battle cry for would-be 'Tiger Mothers' everywhere, and a warning about the emotional rollercoaster ride when you feel you are falling short.**"

— Richard McGregor author of *Asia's Reckoning: China, Japan, and the Fate of US Power in the Pacific Century*

DEAR DIARY BOY

An Exacting Mother, Her Free-Spirited Son, and Their Bittersweet Adventures in an Elite Japanese School

KUMIKO MAKIHARA

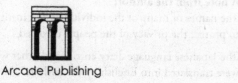

Arcade Publishing

Arcade Publishing books may be purchased in bulk at special discounts for sales promotion, corporate gifts, fund-raising, or educational purposes. Special editions can also be created to specifications. For details, contact the Special Sales Department, Arcade Publishing, 307 West 36th Street, 11th Floor, New York, NY 10018 or arcade@skyhorsepublishing.com.

Arcade Publishing® is a registered trademark of Skyhorse Publishing, Inc.®, a Delaware corporation.

Visit our website at www.arcadepub.com.

10 9 8 7 6 5 4 3 2 1

Library of Congress Cataloging-in-Publication Data is available on file.

Print ISBN: 978-1-950691-61-6
Ebook ISBN: 978-1-62872-892-7

Printed in the United States of America

A note from the author:
The names of many of the individuals and institutions have been changed to protect the privacy of the people involved.

The Japanese language diary entries and other writing excerpts from Taro were translated into English by the author.

Contents

Contents

Foreword

DEAR DIARY BOY BROUGHT BACK A FLOOD of recollections of
my own family's complicated experiences three decades
ago, when we lived in Japan and enrolled our young boys in a
Japanese public school for a year.

Our family and Kumiko's had a surprising amount in common, despite some obvious contrasts. She had been an expatri-
ated Japanese, divorced, and her adopted son, who didn't look
like all the other kids, was from Kazakhstan. We were Amer-
icans, with blond-haired boys, and spoke minimal Japanese.

Unlike Kumiko, all members of our family were totally,
instantly foreign, the biggest factor that affected our every-
day lives. But that foreignness also made our life easier than
Kumiko's. As a Japanese, she was expected to (mostly) be part
of the local culture. Having lived abroad, she was given a bit of
leeway, or at least she had an explanation, for her digressions.
Her safety net, such as it was, was being from an elite, wealthy
family, which gave her some choices and fallback.

For us, there were no expectations (except that we would
always do everything incorrectly). Everyone knew we could not
possibly know the rituals, fall in line with appropriate behavior,
or follow the multitude of rules. All of which applied not only
to the children, but especially to me, as The Mother. Our safety
net: we were not Japanese, and we could bow out if we chose.

Kumiko had enough muscle memory and family support to help her sort her way through school issues and do what she thought was the right thing. But she struggled until the bitter end. (There's a Japanese word for that, without a true English equivalent: *gaman*, which means to keep trying and never stop.)

I would have drowned without Keiko, my one true and genuine friend, who made me her cause that year. She dragged me by the hand, with our kids, to purchase exactly the right items on the lengthy list of precise purchases for backpacks, sports gear, shoes, and earthquake helmets for our boys. And she taught me how to make bento boxes to the best of my ability. And how to: don a kimono for the most serious of ceremonies, sweep our walk, make tea, cook rice, shop wisely, and gift the neighbors.

I remember the day it dawned on my husband and me that we could stop trying to handle every detail of daily life appropriately. Since we were always getting things wrong anyway, we could at least live in a way that was sustainable for us. (A year can be a long time!) They were small things, like how I should hang our laundry on the outdoor line where all could see, but together they grew into a heavy burden. That day, I felt palpably what the phrase "wave of relief" meant.

Being Japanese, Kumiko didn't have that option, and her and her son's strains multiplied, overcoming and squashing mother and son in ways that we were spared because of our foreignness.

In my family, our two very different sons made for a kind of controlled experiment for life in a Japanese school of seven hundred Japanese children plus two foreign boys. Our older son, outgoing and fearless, was placed in a classroom of forty-three children with a young male teacher at the helm who saw this "experiment" as the chance of a lifetime. Our younger son, sensitive and reflective, was placed in a classroom of fifty children (including some with special needs) led by an elderly woman teacher just shy of retirement who saw this "experiment" as, well, too much.

By the end of the school year, our older son graduated from elementary school and transitioned quite happily as he marched off in his Prussian-style uniform to junior high. Our younger son trudged through a zillion repetitions of the times tables but drew the line when his teacher rearranged his "creative" art work, ungluing the grains of rice from his paper and gluing them back in the pattern she wanted. As we watched his spirit fade, we realized we had asked something of him that was just not fair, and he chose to ride out the last few months of the school year shuttling between his sets of grandparents in Florida and California.

I recognize, even with the three decades separating Kumiko's experience and mine, that the thousands of years of small Japanese traditions and big cultural concepts have barely budged.

There is still the sacred and overbearing tradition of mom-meetings for classroom mothers. In my case, I struggled to understand a lot of what was going on, and only several months in did I realize that most of the discussion centered around our son and the ways to have the entire group support him and "this experiment." If he failed, they all failed.

Or the student meetings, when children were left to work out problems within their group, an exercise for a future of collaborative effort. Once, when our older son's class had to divide up into smaller groups for an outing, they spent two and a half days discussing how to divide the number of forty-three children into equal groups to make sure the extra person didn't feel weird or hurt. They finally succeeded.

When I read Kumiko's book, I was shocked again at how—despite globalization over the last thirty years—the Japanese culture still offers little for non-Japanese to grab tightly onto. I deeply appreciate the aesthetic, the order, the trust in doing one's best, the civility of the Japanese. And I realize how hard it remains for outsiders to look deeper than that into the Japanese soul and reach the heart.

—Deborah Fallows is the author of several books, including *Dreaming in Chinese: Mandarin Lessons in Life, Love, and Language*, and most recently *Our Towns: A 100,000-Mile Journey into the Heart of America*

November 16, 2007

I have dreams every day. Scary dreams, fun dreams, all sorts. An example of a scary dream is I was in a war. I killed two people with a sword, but while I was struggling against a third, I lost and died and woke up two days later. In another one, I died and went into a grave, but a friend was already in it.

I don't want to see dreams like that ever again.

A fun dream is like this one. I was jumping up and down on a pancake and moving forward, and then I sunk inside one and got stuck. I came out by eating a pancake that didn't even have any syrup on it.

The Very Beginning

June 3, 1999

• • •

DOCTOR NATALIA GENTLY RESTS HER HAND ON THE BABY'S chest.

"Your new mama and papa are here," she says. The infant slumbers peacefully on his back in the metal crib, his arms outstretched and fingers curled into tiny fists. A piece of wire hangs over one side with a plastic rattle attached: his toy. The tall and slender doctor wears a silver-and-black-stone bracelet with matching earrings. Her dark brown hair is neatly coiffed in a short, fringed cut, and her nails are shaped and manicured. I'm always struck by the elegance and sophistication I come across in these far-flung and poor regions of the former Soviet Union. Natalia slides her hand back and forth to slowly wake the child. He opens his eyes.

•

The entrance to Kokshetau is marked by a roadside sign—a steel structure of the city's name atop two blue triangular frames. To the left is a cemetery; to the right is the town, located in northern Kazakhstan. On our drive through the dusty streets to the maternity hospital we see large gray abandoned buildings with broken or missing windows. On the facade of a tall factory are the words BREAD FOR THE PEOPLE in Russian.

•

"We have lived with him for two weeks and relate to him as our biological son. We believe he also knows us as his mother and father," I say, in the Russian speech I have memorized for the adoption court hearing. I'm so nervous that I have no control over my stiff body, and my words come out in a whisper. But the stenographer is typing. The judge sits with no discernible expression on her face.

A few days later we fly out of Kokshetau on an old Soviet plane that holds about twenty passengers. The rumbling is so loud that I wonder why we are still taxiing until I look out of the window and see that we are airborne. My two-month-old son is sleeping on my lap.

February 13, 2006

When I woke up in the morning, there was a strange letter to me inside my diary. Grandma had drawn a picture of a hungry Diary Boy. Diary Boy is a boy that looks like me.

art by Kikuko Makihara

Yaaay. It's a feast. Hooray!
Today's diary looks yummy!!
(The Japanese character for
word repeatedly fills a bowl with
diary book written across it.)

I
Before

November 1, 2004

• • •

I'M THE ONLY MOTHER ON THE BUS WHO'S NOT WEARING A dark-blue suit. There are six of us pairs—mothers and young children. We pretend not to see each other. But I know. We all have one eye on our kid and the other on our rivals. Taro sits down without offering the seat to me first. And now he's swinging his legs back and forth. The School will be looking for polite and obedient children who reflect good parenting. Have the other mothers noticed our flaws? The competition is going to trump us. Should I have bought a new suit to dress like them instead of making do with this old gray ensemble that has been my go-to suit for all occasions? It's a pleated Issey Miyake blouson and skirt. Stylish and sophisticated, it suits me. But it's not the neat and safe choice that everyone else made. As the bus winds through the urban boulevards, the other moms and kids look serene and confident, focused on their mission ahead of nabbing one of the coveted spots in next year's first grade.

The bus pulls into a wide driveway, lined on both sides by towering elm trees, that leads to The School's dark green iron gate. One by one, in silence, we get off and step into the gentle sunlight of the fall afternoon. Signs guide us to the auditorium where parents are ushered to seats. The kids are lined up and given hanging nametags to slip over their heads. My chest tightens as I watch Taro. A beautiful boy with delicate features, a fair complexion, and silky, chestnut-colored hair, standing so far away from me in formation with the other kids. Five years old and facing a fork in life. Today my beloved will either pass or fail the elementary school exams. As the children march off to their test rooms, we mothers suppress the desire to shout out one more cheer of encouragement to our tiny soldiers.

•

Ojyuken. It means to take a test for kindergarten or primary school. The "o" is an honorific added tongue-in-cheek to the word *jyuken*, or test-taking, to suggest that only members of the upper echelon, big on such polite language, can afford the time and cost to prep a young child for entrance exams and on top of that pay private-school tuition. Taro and I fit that category, mostly. My father is a well-known business executive, and my mother's great grandfather was one of Japan's famed early industrialists, Baron Yataro Iwasaki, for whom Taro was named. (Yataro is Taro's full name.) But I went off script. I married an American. We adopted a baby—a highly unusual act in Japan. My then-husband and I were both working as journalists in Russia when, after I failed to get pregnant and turned forty, we met Taro at a hospital in Kazakhstan. His Kazakh birth mother had left him there a few days after he was born. Taro's porcelain skin tone and light hair suggest his biological father may have been Russian.

Then, three years after we adopted Taro, I left my husband. In normal Tokyo society today, marrying a *gaijin*, or foreigner, and divorce no longer raise eyebrows. But in the exclusive circles of the *ojyuken* world, a single parent is an anomaly and a mixed-race child is unusual. Adoption from a country barely known to most Japanese? Unfathomable. The top schools don't want different. They want high quality predictable.

"Oh. You are on your own?" the woman on the phone from the exam prep school had said to me six months earlier, her voice dropping with disapproval. I had told her I was a busy single parent. That was my excuse for calling so late to inquire about classes. It was already May, and the exams were coming up in November. Most children study for at least two years. We had only six months to go. "A private school might be difficult," she continued.

The world of primary school exams viewed single mothers (and in Japan, it's mostly mothers who raise and educate the kids) as too harried to bring up a child properly and too poor to afford private-school tuition. Besides, how would a working mother manage the logistics of supervising studies and ferrying a child to and from cram school classes? In my Internet searches on *ojyuken*, I came across anxious queries from single mothers about whether private education was beyond their reach. "Can one not enter a private elementary school without a father?" read one entry. "The highly competitive schools or schools for boys and girls of good upbringing would be difficult," came the reply from one exam-info site, adding that for the lower ranked schools, "we don't rule out the possibility."

The test-prep school woman asked me, "Could you move in temporarily with your parents, just until the exams?" I was renting a small apartment near my parents' house that was close enough for Taro to visit them often but far enough away to give me my own space. The woman's reasoning was that if I lived with my parents that would invoke the image of mom and son living comfortably in a suitable house with doting grandparents as opposed to a neglected child and a strapped parent struggling in tiny quarters.

But moving in with my parents wasn't an option. When I left my ex-husband at his posting as a foreign correspondent in Beijing and moved back to Tokyo with Taro, who was then almost three, my parents were perturbed. They were content with their own busy lives. My father was the chairman of a large corporation, and my parents traveled together frequently to overseas conferences. Their nest was brimming without us. My father asked what my plans were going forward, hoping to hear I would be independent. I hadn't thought about my future. I had been preoccupied with my present and past, going over and over the pros and cons of marriage to a man who was talented and engaging, intelligent and articulate, but also volatile, deceitful, and philandering. One day I made my decision, packed up, and flew home with Taro with no idea about what to do next.

"I just can't understand what you're thinking," my father had grumbled.

"No," I told the woman. "It's not possible to move in with my parents."

Why was I even considering a private school? It had been a last-minute notion. As one of those harried single moms,

I hadn't given Taro's schooling much thought. After returning to Japan, I had started working as an assistant to the president of a large hotel complex in the south of Japan, and I traveled nearly every week between Tokyo and the resort, a ninety-minute plane ride away. My mind was consumed on the logistics of whether to take Taro with me on these trips or leave him with my parents when they were home. Taro attended a neighborhood day care center, and nearly all of the children there would go on to the local public school, a well-regarded one in an affluent district that I myself had attended. I had always assumed that I would send Taro there, too.

Japan has a well-respected public education system that emphasizes a high-level standardized curriculum and a belief that all children have the same potential to learn. There are no gifted tracks in public primary schools that go from grade one through six. Elementary school education also stresses character building alongside academics, instructing children to get along with others, clean their surroundings and respect their teachers and the environment. Traditionally, only the uber-elite, wealthy, or particularly ambitious families opted out of public schools in their children's early years. Just about one percent of Japanese primary school children attend private schools. I certainly didn't want to segregate Taro at such a young age into that privileged minority.

But when Taro's piano teacher heard of my intentions, she urged me to reconsider my apparently simplistic reasoning. I was surprised to find that most of my supposedly liberal and open-minded friends agreed with her, too. Public schools aren't what they used to be, they all said, citing declining academic levels, demoralized teachers, and sub-standard facilities. Indeed, the share of students going to private junior high schools, which start at seventh grade, has been steadily on the rise. About seven percent of Japanese children now attend private secondary schools because their parents believe that they offer higher-quality teaching and help pave the way for entry into prestigious high schools and universities.

"Get your foot in the door early," was the common chorus I heard from our piano teacher and my friends. I should aim for a private school with an affiliated upper school that Taro could matriculate into. They argued that it would be easier to prep children for private school entrance exams while they were still young and could be cajoled by their mothers, not to mention the fact that the tests would get more difficult down the line. Well, why not then? What did I have to lose anyway, especially if I had the good public school as a backup? I wasn't familiar with even the names of the private schools, so I just picked my father's alma mater, The School, assuming that legacy would help us. The School had the reputation of being one of the country's highest-level elementary schools, both academically and athletically. At the least we could do what some parents called *kinen juken* or commemorative exam-taking; taking the test for the hell of it to have the experience of getting dressed up and stepping into the hallowed halls of prestigious schools. And anyway, how hard could a test for five- and six-year-olds be? I was already picturing myself bantering happily with other *ojyuken* moms, our high-achieving children by our sides.

•

I walk gingerly over to a group of parents sitting in the back of the room at an exam prep school. Taro is having a trial class.

The cram school is checking him out before offering enrollment. They *don't* want a kid who will disrupt the class. They *do* want a kid who will get into a good school so they can boast about that in their brochures. I take a seat at the end of the parents' row and pray that Taro will sit through class obediently. I see him eyeing this new, hushed environment. The other children, about ten of them, are already practice-dressed for exam day, wearing white polo shirts and navy-blue shorts or skirts. They sit with backs straight, hands on their laps and papers in the middle of their desks with two sharpened pencils to the right, lead facing forward. Taro's hands dangle by his sides. A matronly teacher walks in. "Where is your pencil, Taro?" she asks. He breaks into a coy smile and pulls one out from behind his ear. The teacher laughs. I suppress a grin. The other parents remain silent.

"What happens from here depends on how much effort the mother puts in," the teacher tells me in her office after class. In other words, how quickly can I bring Taro up to speed on the drill sheets, and can I whip him into shape to sit through the hour-long written test and to perform in the group behavior exams? Suddenly, Taro, who had been instructed to stay in the adjacent room, comes bounding in and jumps onto my lap, his dirty sneakers touching the sofa's edge along the way. When I tell him to wait until I finish talking, he repeatedly shouts in English, "Excuse me, Mama," so happy to try out the phrase I had just taught him to use when interrupting adults. Since our move back from Beijing to Tokyo, Taro had lost the Chinese he had learned there from his nanny and the English he had spoken with his Dad and spoke only Japanese now, so I had been trying to re-teach him English, phrase by phrase. But right now, the focus is on the wild boy in the civilized cram school. I can't yell at him because then I'd come across as an out-of-control parent. The teacher gives us a cold and knowing smile, and we leave as quickly as possible. My heart is heavy, but Taro is high from his release. He holds my hand and pulls ahead, and I can feel the skip in his step.

The exam prep schools are called *juku*, and they are part of the boundless, multi-billion-dollar *ojyuken* industry that converts every parental anxiety into a business opportunity. In addition to the cram schools and tutoring services, children can sharpen their test skills at mock examinations and overnight study retreats. Department stores sell an array of exam-appropriate clothing and accessories. There are the conservative dark-blue suits and dresses for moms, some with discreet pockets to store an amulet from a temple purported to protect the bearer and bring good fortune. There are foldable slippers to wear in classrooms since outdoor shoes are removed at schools. You can always borrow from the school's supply, but that signals to everyone how careless you were to forget your own. There are dark-blue umbrellas with fitted carry bags to place them in so you don't drip rainwater on the floor of your dream school, and tiny cotton covers to elegantly couch tissue packs. (Every child is expected to have tissues in one pocket and a handkerchief in the other.) Bookstores have shelves devoted to drill books, school rankings, samples of previous test questions, and how-to-publications with titles like *The 125 Things You Need to Know About Elementary School Entrance Exams*.

After several rejections, we finally found a *juku* that would take us in. A mother from Taro's soccer class had felt sorry for me and referred us to the cram school her son attended. *Sakura*, which means "cherry blossom," was located in a dark studio apartment in an aging building one block back from a busy city street.

"It's really too late," said the principal who appeared to be in her sixties. "But I guess if you are Matsui-san's introduction I will have to accept you."

She handed me an invoice for seven-hundred dollars to cover registration, one month's tuition, textbooks, and utilities. There was also a sheet that listed the *juku* rules that included this entry: "*If Sakura concludes that the mother is emotionally unstable, we will ask you to withdraw.*"

Taro began attending Sakura twice a week. The cram school's touted "private instruction" meant three teachers, each seated in front of a single student, squeezed into one of the two small rooms going over drill sheets and sample tests. Most schools gave athletic exams, too, and for that practice the teacher would gauge Taro's coordination in the same tiny room, instructing for example, "Hop in one place on your left foot!" and count, stopwatch in hand, while he bobbed up and down next to a desk, his pageboy-style hair fluttering about.

Each school administers its own unique exams, but they generally include written, art, athletic, and behavioral components— plus an interview. The written tests have a variety of formats. In listening comprehension, children hear a recording of a story followed by questions. For example, they might hear:

Hanako-san went to meet her father. At the crosswalk, she passed a man wearing a white hat. There was a man wearing a sweater and glasses sitting on a park bench. A man wearing a tie got off the bus. There was a man with a mustache by the mailbox. Her father was waiting at the train station.

Which one is Hanako-san's father? [1]

And then be shown a picture of five men, each dressed differently. One is wearing a white hat, two have glasses, another has a tie and another a mustache. The kids would have to remember that the dad had none of those and select the figure not wearing any of those items.

That's actually an extremely short example. Many recorded stories run for about five minutes, and the children don't take notes. While some of the five- and six-year-old examinees have already been taught by their parents to read and write, the tests are administered on the premise that the children are not yet literate. They respond by marking the illustration that corresponds to the right answer. Listening comprehension turned out to be Taro's strongest area.

The other tests were even more challenging, such as those to discern and predict patterns. Here's one where you have to figure out where the circles would go in the one blank box.[2]

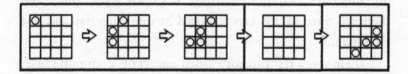

1 *TV Asahi*, "Tenka no Tatsujin" http://www.nikken-net.com/qa/

2 Exzam Inc., "Shogakko Jyukenmondaishu Jitsuryoku 23 sample questions." https://www.exzam.co.jp/sample_downloads4.html (Japanese)

To solve this, you have to deduce that all of the circles are shifting to the right, then notice that, in the final box, one circle has been added to the bottom row. With that pattern in mind, the correct answer would be:

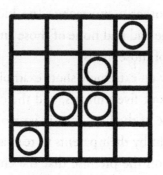

Many tests assumed an understanding of scientific concepts well beyond the child's age level. How does the level of liquid in a glass change if you put blocks inside? After putting a sugar cube in different amounts of water, which drink is the sweetest? How many eggs remain if a farmer removes one on rainy days, two on sunny days, none when it's cloudy, and there are three sunny days followed by one rainy day and one cloudy one?

There was a test category called *joshiki* or "common sense" with various sub-sections like "common sense about nature" or "common sense of the seasons" in which children needed to match rice-planting and swallows' nests with springtime and watermelons and cicadas with the summer. In one nature category question, children are shown an illustration of five flowers: tulips, a hyacinth, a morning glory, crocuses, and daffodils. They must then choose an odd one out.[3]

The correct answer is the morning glory because it's the only one that grows from a seed rather than a bulb. "Remember Taro, there're seven dots on a ladybug," a teacher shouted after us as we were leaving class one day. Most urbanites had to learn such nature trivia from books, although the more motivated *ojyuken* parents arranged study trips to the countryside or sent their children to sleepover cram camps in rural areas.

Most nerve-wracking for parents was the "common sense on daily life" category that tested manners and housekeeping skills, both reflecting how the child had been raised and exposing any slovenly habits learned at home. Taro got a C in table setting on one practice test because "he tossed all of the plates when distributing them," according to the teacher's report. "Please have him actually set the table at home for review." Ouch! The test was a referendum on my parenting skills, and I'd been caught out. It was true that after an exhausting day I would lay the spread myself at full speed (maybe I *was* tossing plates?) rather than let Taro help me. And now we would both pay the price for my impatience.

In one session, the children were put into groups and given a picnic sheet, a large bottle of tea, a box of cookies and some cups and plates. They were expected to serve each other

3 Exzam Inc., "Shogakko Jyukenmondaishu Jitsuryoku 23 sample questions." https://www.exzam.co.jp/sample_downloads4.html (Japanese)

politely and insist that others eat and drink before them, just as well-mannered Japanese adults do so endlessly. The schools were looking for kids not just clever on paper but also polite and considerate. Any number of these tasks could appear in an exam. And the mothers had to polish their products by November.

The art tests assessed proficiency in drawing pictures and making crafts, many of which were tedious, presumably to test patience and dexterity. Taro loathed *chigiri-e*, a traditional Japanese art where pictures are created by gluing hand-torn pieces of fibrous *washi* paper onto a sheet.

"You mustn't just rip the paper," the Sakura principal told Taro, holding up a purple sheet to demonstrate.

"You have to use your nails to carefully, gently tear away the pieces," she said, as she creased a line down the paper with her nails. *Origami*, an examiner's favorite, was another weak area for my restless boy. While other children could quickly produce cranes (nineteen folds) and water lilies (twenty-eight folds), Taro, after months, mastered only the piano (ten folds) and the peasant (twelve folds without the trousers). His crayon sketch of a blue train on gray grass—an unschooled depiction of a family trip to northern Japan—earned a D-minus on a practice test. My five-year-old's GPA was already plummeting.

The sports section judged skills like jumping rope, bouncing a ball, skipping, and other agile maneuvers. Being athletic, Taro did well on these, but the tests posed the additional challenge of how well children could follow and remember instructions. There could be a complicated obstacle course where, for example, you twirl a hula hoop twice, then dribble a ball up to one goal, and from there hop to the next destination.

In the group activity screening, the children would be divided into teams and told to solve a task together. They might be given some paper, chopsticks, wire, glue, and scissors and be asked to make a pond and pretend they are fishing. Perhaps there would be fewer tools than children to see how well they shared, and schools were always watching to see how the kids handled equipment. Do you give the scissors to your friend with the blades facing respectfully toward you rather than pointing dangerously at the recipient? Do you pass things on politely using both hands? And when you are done do you leave everything on the floor, which suggests that at home mom puts away the toys, or do you gather them neatly in a corner, revealing a good upbringing?

"You see?" I remember saying to Taro in one of our typical attempts at tackling Sakura's daily homework assignments. For what seemed like the tenth time that evening, I shoved a baseball cap sideways on Taro's head and pointed to the mirror that I had placed before him. "The brim is on the opposite side." We were practicing a test question where the children would be shown a picture of a reflection in a mirror of a child wearing a cap sideways and then presented with two pictures of the same child but with the brims in different directions. Which is the accurate reflection? I wasn't trying to explain scientific theory. I just wanted Taro to memorize that reflections appear opposite so he could check the correct box on the test. But Taro never got it. He barely knew right from left, for that matter. I couldn't think of a way to get Taro to master this question other than to repeat the process over and over again. Show him the mirror, point to the brim on his head, point to the brim in the mirror, exclaim with enthusiasm that the brim appears in the opposite direction in reflections.

To my growing irritation, Taro didn't seem to be trying. He squirmed in his chair, dangled his legs, slumped over on the table, and shouted out any answer.

"This one!" I was momentarily thrilled with a correct reply, only to realize he had made a lucky guess.

"Look carefully. Don't you get it?" I shouted, forcefully pressing the cap down on his head.

"I quit!" Taro said and raced out of the room. I ran after him and grabbed him and dragged him back to the table. It was like this nearly every time.

•

Sakura's principal became increasingly high-strung the closer it got to November. She disapproved of our plans to spend the month of July in New York City. My brother and his family lived there, and I had arranged for us to stay in his apartment while they were away for the summer. I had enrolled Taro in a day camp to expose him to the English language and another culture. From the principal's point of view, such ventures only detracted from exam prep.

"They say you should do as many drill sheets as your height when they are piled up," she told me. "But I don't think you will be able to."

She handed me an exercise book to take with us that was less than one inch thick. Still, that would be enough to send the daggers flying. Every morning after breakfast I would try to coax Taro into doing a few sheets. I could spend two fruitless hours trying to teach him a concept like recognizing the hidden components in a drawing of a pile of building blocks. That type of question required children to figure out the number of blocks in the rear of a three-dimensional pile that weren't directly visible in the picture. I would display some real blocks and walk Taro around them to show him the different perspectives. Like the baseball cap reflection, he couldn't grasp the notion, and we would end up in an angry standoff with scuffles and chases around the apartment. Each day we left the apartment ragged, and I worried that Taro might take his frustrations out by pummeling a campmate.

I felt sick with panic when I thought about how much Taro didn't know and very likely wouldn't ingest by exam day. Whenever we faced a new task, I wondered why a child needed to master it to enter elementary school. But I ignored my own questions and lamented Taro's inabilities. I lay low and ran with the herd. Why wasn't I standing tall and judging my son on his own merits? I was educated and worldly, after all. More than a decade older than most of the other *ojyuken* moms who were in their twenties and thirties, I had enjoyed a far more varied life. As far as I could tell, most of them had held one job out of school and then stopped working when they had children to devote themselves to homemaking and child-rearing, which is a typical life pattern for Japanese women. I had lived in cities around the world and worked as a foreign correspondent for *Time Magazine* in Tokyo and in Russia as a Features Editor at the *Moscow Times*. You would have expected me to have a broader and wiser perspective. But instead I had tunnel vision. I was obsessed with making sure I had the correct tissue pack cover. I measured Taro by the stick of the cram school, and I was sinking deeper every day into the quicksand of exam hell.

I attribute my ultra-compliance to Japanese social mores to three things: my personality, my upbringing, and Japan's conformist culture. I've always been hyper-vigilant and prone to free-wheeling fantasy. Like I'll notice a shard of glass on the sidewalk, and next thing I'll imagine the prick and pain of it piercing my bare foot and see the thick ooze of deep-red blood. In my early childhood spent in the suburbs of London where my father's job had taken us, my busy mind was happy. My bountiful observations were rich fodder for make-believe with my older brother, our friends, and my dolls. And my flights of fancy always had a safe place to return to, the unwavering base of the familiar: the small private school I attended from age three, my own bedroom upstairs in our two-story house in Purley with lawns in the front and back, and the blue and white Triumph coupe in which my mother drove me to school and my ballet and piano lessons. This secure existence shattered at age eight when my father's employer ordered him to transfer back to Tokyo. On that sunny morning, my brother, who was nine, and I had been studying the rips in the dining room wallpaper, suspected to be the mischief of a squirrel, when my father announced we were moving back to the hometown I had left when I was one.

"What's Japan like?" I asked.

"It's wonderful," my father said. "Everything will be great."

One month later my brother and I were trudging along a dirt road in the city of Kawasaki, just south of Tokyo, following a group of neighborhood children to our new school. We had moved into a small three-room apartment as the housing situation in Japan was far below the standards of England. We didn't know the route to school yet around the open sewers, rice paddies, and tiny houses with corrugated aluminum roofs. Once there, groups of kids would surround me and finger my clothes and mimic my replies to their questions. The girls tugged at the straps of my British, navy-wool jumper skirt so unlike like the thin cotton ones they wore.

"My English is better than my Japanese," one of them would say in a low tone, mocking my deep voice. I had told them that in the hopes that they would be forgiving about any mistakes I made in Japanese. But I soon learned that in Japan, anything different—from clothes to speech—would be pointed out as a reason for exclusion. And everyone always seemed to be with someone else, whether to walk to the bathroom or play during recess. Even tag was played as chain tag where you hold hands once you are caught so that "it" was a group of kids rather than an individual.

Confused and miserable, every day after school I came home and cried and complained to my mother that no one liked me.

"Just try to be like everyone else," she advised. "Don't say you speak English. It makes you sound snobbish and makes people jealous."

The singular message from my parents was that Japan was a great place that I should accept and acquiesce to and never question. That would take a blind leap of faith coming from a private school in tranquil and verdant Purley to a public school in the smog-engulfed industrial city of Kawasaki in the late 1960s.

Japan felt rough and dirty. In England, school assembly meetings had taken place indoors, where we sat at our desks or on the bleachers. In Japan, the morning gatherings were outside, and everyone stood at attention, facing a podium from where teachers made speeches and announcements. During the hot and humid summer months, students sometimes fainted or even vomited. The drama of someone suddenly collapsing frightened me. Even more disturbing was the nonchalant reaction of the teachers and other students who mechanically assisted the child to his or her feet and casually kicked sand to cover the retch.

The British school looked like an old mansion, and the bathrooms were cozy little rooms down the hallway with chains hanging from a tank above to flush. My Japanese school was a standard, three-story cement block building and had pit toilets where the dark and smelly shafts seemed to go down forever and were the source of horror stories like the one of a ghost girl who had fallen in long ago and still lived down there. At recess in England we polished chestnut seeds called conkers and ran around an asphalt playground with a climbing structure and slide. In Japan, the kids played fierce dodgeball, and the girls competed in Chinese jump rope, a complex game of skipping around a long band of elastic, on a dusty playing field. I hated all the contrasts and yearned for my room in Purley while I sat in the tiny bedroom I now shared with my brother and sucked on the dwindling supply of fruit pastilles that we had brought back from England.

Desperate to make friends, I followed my parents' advice. I watched, absorbed, and copied. I wore hand-me-downs from an older cousin—cotton skirts and blouses that had small embroidered flowers like the ones on the other girls' clothes. "Can I play?" I timidly asked as I lined up to try a turn at jumping up to the elastic band. If anyone commented on my anomalies, I responded with a silent, stoic smile and waited for the moment to pass. As I endured I began to blend in, and, just as my parents had said, I was accepted. This acquiesce-and-join strategy has remained my modus operandi ever since.

In the *ojyuken* world this meant do as the other young moms do and mold Taro into a clone of one of their kids.

•

In September, two months before the exams, I enrolled Taro in a second cram school that was well known for athletic test prep and its thirty-something male teacher, whom the mothers certified a "charisma coach" for the hold he had on his pupils. I dutifully followed the other moms when they went into groupie mode and crowded around coach's parked car to examine the SUV's model and the type of car seats he had for his kids. The teacher's control over the students was impressive, as was the discipline and agility of the children. If the teacher shouted, "crocodile!" the forty or so children instantly dropped down prone on the gleaming gymnasium floor and crawled forward, leaning on forearms to pull themselves ahead. They looked like little Navy SEALs-in-training. In addition to crocodile, there were bear, seal, rabbit, and frog movements that apparently each displayed an aspect of strength and coordination for examiners to judge.

Shortly after he started the class, Taro tried to get other kids to join him in clowning around, making silly poses when he should have been standing straight and waiting for the next command. Such class clowning had always elicited giggles from his friends at day care, but here, no one was enticed. The teacher asked him, "Yataro-kun.[4] Do you want to be part of this exercise? Are you ready to join us?" Charisma coach's tone was calm, but being singled out in front of the large group appeared to overwhelm Taro. He stood stiffly and managed a tiny nod as tears welled up in his eyes. From the parents' observation section in the bleachers, I ached for his embarrassment. And also for my own.

The sports *juku* gave me a list of sixty things Taro should master. It included items like skipping rhythmically, doing consecutive somersaults, bouncing a ball twenty times in a row, and more complex stunts like walking across a balance beam holding a ladle with a ball in it. Further, to show good upbringing, Taro should know how to fold pajamas while ironing out any creases by hand, separate garbage for recycling, wring out all the droplets from a wet hand towel, hang laundry with clothespins, and tie a bow. Taro could manage a very loose bow but certainly not without looking, a feat some schools were rumored to require. One desperate mother wrote to a chat room devoted to entrance examinations that her son had not mastered tying his apron behind his back: "We have tried several times, but each time cannot do it and get so disheartened." Her woes prompted one empathetic mother to share the joy of her own son's triumph: "My son also couldn't do it so we trained hard . . . just last night at dinner when he was helping out, he was suddenly wearing an apron. I thought, 'no way,' but looked in the back, and the bow was there. I was so moved I

---

4 *Kun* is an honorific title usually used among males.

hugged him." Only in this frenzied *ojyuken* world could apron strings stir up such passion.

One evening, I was surprised to receive a call at home from Sakura's principal.

"I've just received the questions for tomorrow's test," she said breathlessly. "I can fax them to you."

I was taken aback. I had signed Taro up, at her urging, to take a two-hour-long practice entrance exam held nationwide. Wasn't this to gauge Taro's current strengths and weaknesses so we could strategize? Didn't seeing the questions in advance defeat that purpose? And moreover, isn't that cheating? From her tone, I got the sense that she expected me to be grateful and happy, so I tried as politely as I could to broach just the subject of the point of taking the test while knowing the content in advance. The principal explained that she was worried that Taro might get upset if there were too many questions he couldn't answer, and that might prompt him to act up and cause a commotion that would reflect badly on Sakura. For a few minutes, I paced around the fax machine in my cramped study in our apartment, wondering what I should do. Then, in a rare moment of clarity, I came to my senses. Of course I shouldn't show Taro the questions. It's hard enough to teach honesty to a child without making little exceptions along the way. Why would I tell a child who hadn't even started school yet to cheat on a test?

"This is just a practice," I told Taro. "So it's OK if you don't know the right answers. Just answer the ones you can."

Early the next morning, we headed to the campus of Tokyo's Sophia University. Hundreds of other parents and children were there, many of them dressed in their exam-day outfits. We were told to take our kids to the designated lecture halls and find them seats. One girl was sobbing while her increasingly exasperated mother tried to coax her to sit down. I felt sorry for them as their tension spiraled upward with the mother's frustration upsetting her daughter even more.

"Don't kick the seat in front of you during the test," I told Taro.

Once the children were settled into what was likely the biggest classroom they had ever seen, the parents were guided to an auditorium where a former private school teacher gave a talk on filling out application forms and interview techniques. I came away with several good tips. One was to fill out school documents (which were expected to be handwritten) in faint pencil first, then trace over your draft with a fountain pen, let dry and erase any remaining pencil marks. That way you avoided making mistakes in pen. The speaker also advised single parents being interviewed to come clean right away on that liability. "Just explain, before you take your seat, that you are divorced and therefore had to come to the interview alone," she said.

After the test, the parents and kids streamed out of the campus and back toward the local train station. I was relieved and impressed to see that the children all appeared quite normal—healthily rambunctious, running around, and making new friends—despite their high-stress circumstances. Taro confessed to me that he and a boy he befriended had been scolded for not quieting down quickly enough after a break.

"The teacher said, 'I'm going to send you home if you don't settle down,' but me and another boy said, 'We know she's never gonna do that,'" he told me.

Two weeks later, the Sakura principal handed me a manila envelope with the test results. Her eyes were cast down in sympathy and discomfort for bearing bad news.

"It's a bit disappointing, but there is still some time," she said. Taro had ranked 1,363rd out of 1,381 examinees. He took one more practice exam a few months later and came out even worse at 1,615th place out of 1,621.

On that second test, Taro scored a two out of a possible thirty points on the art section. The task was to create an Olympic medal out of two sheets of paper. Each sheet had a circle printed on it, one slightly larger than the other. The larger one was to be the rim of the medal. The other was to be the medal itself and should be cut out and pasted inside the rim. Taro had colored over the outline of the rim in red, using a lot of crayon with lines jutting in and out of the circle. Inside his medal, he drew a crude but clearly detectable child playing soccer: a boy in a blue shirt with stick legs kicking a black and white ball. There was a wavy green line of rolling hills in the background. He taped a green ribbon at the top of the medal to be its chain, but he didn't get around to cutting the medal out and gluing it into its rim. Still, should his efforts have merited only two points? The examiners probably saw a slapdash illustration with no scale or perspective and an incomplete project. At the time, I agreed with their assessment and despaired over Taro's failure. Couldn't he have kept the coloring within the borders? Why didn't the legs have any feet or the head any hair? But years later when I look at his drawing, I see Taro thinking about his own blue soccer jersey and the black and white ball that he kicked at a summer camp in the mountains north of Tokyo. The boy in the drawing has a wide smile with lips drawn twice, first in black and then in red.

•

Throughout the summer and fall, the private schools held campus tours. Sakura advised us to arrive early, remember our slippers and sign in at the registration desk in neat handwriting. I visited The School in September. About a thousand of us parents sat in the auditorium along with a few children scattered about. Some parents claim they want their kids to have a first-hand look to see if the school is a fit, but many of us, including me, would never take along our children for fear of having a boisterous child at our side. The schools may or may not be observing and pre-screening at these events, but it's likely that they *would* take note of an unruly child. The School showed a film from a summer retreat, and the principal gave a talk about the institution's history and commitment to each child. Afterward, there was a question-and-answer session. Q-and-As are usually staid affairs in Japan because people are reluctant to ask questions that could make them stand out in a crowd or appear too forward in the culture that values modesty. So here again, there were just a few polite inquiries. Then, one girl, she had to be either five or six years old as a potential examinee, stood up and spoke distinctly into the microphone: "Do you have calligraphy classes? Because I like calligraphy."

I doubt I was the only one in the audience whose stomach churned in resentment at the image of a child quietly writing characters with inked brush. She had just raised the bar higher for all of us.

During the final two months before the exams, I increased Taro's lessons at Sakura to three afternoons a week to drill for the written test, craft-making, and interviews and continued with the sports class on Saturdays. Sakura's principal was pleased with my financial commitment and pressured another mother to up the frequency of her child's classes by pointing to me and saying, "Makihara-san over here started late, so now she's coming three times a week."

On workdays, I often relied on my mother and baby sitters to deliver Taro to and from the cram schools, and when I could manage the time off, rushed in at the end of class when the teachers summarized the day's lesson and offered advice to parents.

"Don't take such a big bag to the test," one teacher told me, gesturing toward my briefcase. A dark-blue or black handbag plus tote were preferred. Sakura's principal suggested that I take Taro out of day care until the exams were over, explaining that many children studied full-time during the last lap.

"And you know, day care is not regarded well. Children just play wildly there," she said, waving her hands in the air to stress the chaos.

She was reinforcing the stereotype that day care—which caters to working mothers in Japan—is rough-and-tumble and inferior to private kindergartens for the more civilized children of full-time mothers. But withdrawal was not going to be an option for us with my full-time job.

Oblivious to all of this grown-up circumspection, Taro dutifully allowed himself to be ferried back and forth to his classes. Sakura had a box full of tiny glass animals from which the children got to take one reward home after each class. Taro always spent a good few minutes perusing the menagerie before making that difficult choice. My mother, being a grandmother, treated him every time she picked him up with a visit to a nearby traditional Japanese cake shop where they ate bean paste treats and sipped green tea. On the weekends, I would ride my bike, with Taro in the back, up the long hill to the sports school. Despite all, still a happy child, he would cheer me on, shouting rhythmically to my pedal pushing, "*Gambare, gambare, Maaaaama*" or "Go, go, Moooooom," squeezing my waist with his small hands.

•

"Isn't this fun? I'm applying to twelve schools," a mother I had met at the sports class told me about a month before the exams when we had coffee at a nearby Denny's while the kids were in session. That's a lot of work since most applications require an essay by the parents as well as detailed family background information, all of which should be handwritten without any mistakes. The walls were closing in on many of the *ojyuken* mothers around me, some of whom were taking measures that, in my opinion, bordered on the mental danger zone shunned by Sakura. In one after-class session, a teacher lectured mothers who listened earnestly about recommended good-luck charms, which are ubiquitous in the superstitious Japanese culture, to carry on exam days. They ranged from the ordinary amulets from temples to the bizarre-but worked-for-one-family-in-the-past objects like the lid of a teapot. I couldn't believe I was sitting through a serious discussion about stashing a teapot lid in my pocket on exam day, and paying for this advice, too. But if I expressed such thoughts, I'd be the one deemed crazy for not exploring every single possible route to success. Acquiesce and join.

Shortly before the exams, our craft teacher told a group of mothers, "Please remember that these children have only been in this world for a short five years. If they fail, please blame yourselves." I was moved nearly to tears. But the reaction of the other moms was hostile.

"What was *that* about?" they protested, suspicious that the young woman teacher was preparing to skirt responsibility for any failures. In an interview prep session at Sakura, a teacher asked the children to name what they had eaten for breakfast.

"Stir-fried beef and peppers," said one child.

That was frowned upon as a revelation that the mother was heating up last night's leftovers.

"Yogurt, a kiwi, bread. Oh, and a prune. And cheese," Taro answered.

"That is an excellent breakfast, everyone," the teacher exalted. "The school will think, '*There* is a wonderful mother.'"

I felt the temperature rise in my beaming cheeks as I basked in the satisfaction of being praised before a room of stay-at-home moms. I wanted the world to know that a single, working parent could produce just as strong a little test taker. The teacher then asked the children when their mothers scolded them. She cited as a bad example, one child's reply of "When I puff on a cigarette my mom left in the ashtray."

"When does your mother praise you?" the teacher continued, pointing to one boy.

"When I pass the entrance exam," he answered.

I asked Taro the same question later at home. He raised his voice to reply in the appropriate formal and polite manner: "When I give the correct response about breakfast."

The School's application form asked about the child's strengths and weaknesses and for an essay on why the parents were choosing this school. I described Taro's love of books and the outdoors and our connections to The School with my father being a graduate. (Although I had also found out that The School was famous for not being generous with legacy. A relative of the head of the board, for example, had recently been denied entry.) And I wrote openly about our family background. Yes, I was divorced. On top of that, Taro was adopted. Sakura's principal, who read all of our application essays, urged me to remove the mention of divorce and adoption because she said neither would be taken in a positive light. I knew that the adoption would be befuddling. I had stopped discussing it in Japan after I found that people either reacted with embarrassment, feeling they had pried a dark secret out of me, or they regarded me as a do-gooder who wanted to save a child.

"Do you work for an NGO or something?" the director of Taro's day care center had asked me when I explained his background to her. I compromised on the divorce by rewording the sentence to say only that we lived alone, but I left the adoption in there. For once, my attitude was cavalier. If The School rejected us for that, so be it. I had not lost sight of the fact that the adoption was a pillar of our family history, and we would probably not be happy in a school that would not accept Taro's heritage.

•

"How was the test?" I asked Taro after the children were paraded back into the auditorium on The School's first exam day.

"Easy," he said. My heart sank. It couldn't possibly have been a simple exam, so he must have misunderstood the instructions. The only test details I could wrangle out of him were that the children had been told to fold origami during a break and that he had made the peasant. Two days later, we returned for the second part: the parents' interview and the children's group activity behavioral test. The initial gathering area in the school cafeteria was packed with hundreds of primly dressed children and mothers, this time all accompanied by their husbands. It was all hands on deck for the big day. I wondered if Taro noticed that we were the only pair among all the threesomes. I ran into a woman from a PR firm we had hired at the resort I worked for. I had sat through several of her PowerPoint presentations. Here she was in a dark suit, a handsome husband by her side, and a poised daughter. We smiled politely at each other and said nothing, but volumes of information flew between us: *So all that time you had this double life, sending your child to cram school, prepping for the exams. Now, we are rivals.*

The children were ushered off to their tests, and the parents were assigned to seats in classrooms to wait to be called for their interviews. When my turn came and I opened the door to the interview room, I was struck by how young the three male teachers sitting at the other end appeared. While preparing for the exams I had come to view things from Taro's perspective and had begun to look up to all teachers as my seniors. The revelation of my advanced age relaxed me and prompted me to speak perhaps too frankly.

"I see that Taro likes soccer," one teacher said, peering down at my application.

"Do you play together with him?" he asked.

"Oh no, I just send him to a clinic," I replied, and then immediately regretted it, thinking that made me sound like an uninvolved mother.

But I managed to get back in the groove with the next question.

"What considerations do you have in raising Yataro?" an examiner asked.

"He needs to be strong to survive societal prejudices," I said. "But I hope he can also, because of his background, understand the pain of others and be that much kinder."

After the interviews, we waited in the classrooms for our children to be brought to us. "Stop that. It's dangerous," we overheard a teacher scolding a child. Taro later told me that it had been him. He had been pulling on the strap of his name tag, pretending it was a noose and acting as if he were choking.

Two days later, I went to The School again, this time on my own. The registration numbers of successful applicants would be posted on a large glass-encased board by the campus entrance. As the bus drew near the school I saw a few dour-faced mothers walking on the street, some in tears. Others clutched large envelopes, the signs of victory as the packets contained matriculation information. It was a surreal walk from the bus stop along the tree-lined path, passing by the elated and the crushed, as I avoided eye contact and respected space for the joy and grief. I overheard one father say to his daughter, "Congratulations. Now you can go back to kinder-garten tomorrow."

Afraid to know, I looked up at the board. It was there. Taro's number. Just to make sure, I snapped a photo of it with my phone. Somehow, we had made it. I would never know why. A relief and a thrill. But the excitement quickly transformed into a nagging sense of worry. What had I done?

December 30, 2005

Yesterday I got a 2-centimeter shell. It is pretty after I washed it. But I also have other stones and small shells. I washed the round shell, but it still has a sandy feeling inside. This is how I get them. First the wave comes, and after the sand goes wild like inside miso soup, you can see stones and shells. Then you grab them quickly. When I got one, I said, "Yes!" After that I took it and showed it to Mama. She said she wanted to make a necklace with it. I said "OK."

II
Getting There

April 6, 2005

• • •

Taro's first day of school. The 112 little survivors of the exams can now don the coveted uniforms. For the boys, a dark-blue Prussian-collar jacket with shorts and a cap. For the girls, a dark-blue sailor-suit top with a red bow and pleated skirt. On a balmy spring morning, the children, assembled in pairs of boys and girls holding hands in their stiff new wear, marched down a cherry tree-lined path to the auditorium for the enrollment ceremony that would mark their new lives. They would now be in school every weekday, with just one month off in the summer and two weeks off in spring and in winter. The older students stood on both sides of the lane, clapping and cheering as the first graders paraded beneath a soft canopy of pink blossoms. As they entered the hall, the sixth-grade orchestra performed "Pomp and Circumstance."

"The cherry trees began to flower splendidly as if they were really waiting for you," the principal said in his greeting. There were four classes: east, west, north, and south. Taro was in First

Grade South, headed by homeroom teacher Mori Sensei,[5] a mid-forties, soft-spoken man with curly hair and wire-rimmed glasses. In the airy classroom with neatly aligned individual desks, Mori Sensei welcomed his twenty-eight new students with a song, accompanying himself on the guitar. He then circulated a small box.

"If you open the lid of the box carefully, you will see a picture of someone Sensei really likes," he said. Taro peered into the box and smiled when he saw his reflection in the tiny mirror pasted inside.

The parents' first day of school had been a few months earlier when we attended the inaugural parent-teacher meeting for incoming first graders. I put on my usual gray pleated ensemble and headed to The School by train and bus. As I got closer to campus, I scanned my surroundings for any formally dressed, dark-suited women. Who could be a potential friend or ally? Who should I be wary of? A club of 112 mothers (fathers were a rare sight at these meetings) was forming, and the scramble for a secure position was underway. I approached some moms while walking up the driveway from the bus stop to the school gate. Eye contact followed by a slight bow of the head with a deferential smile. That's how the connections start. Introduction is by way of your child's name.

"I am the mother of Yataro Makihara," I would say. The Japanese proverb goes, "The capable eagle hides its talons," and these mothers were smart. So after the greetings came the self-deprecating assessments of their children, like "my son is so unruly," or "you wouldn't believe how spaced-out my daughter is." That wasn't so difficult for me since I felt I could honestly

---

5 *Sensei* means "teacher," and the children referred to their teachers by their last names followed by the title of sensei, or simply as sensei.

say, "I don't know how Taro passed the exam." What was trickier was undermining my career. Only a minority of mothers had professions, and their self-introductions included regret that their work might interfere with parental school duties.

"I have a job, so I'm worried," several of them said, looking earnestly anxious but also hopeful they might form some sort of alliance amongst themselves. I would have liked to join that group, but it was hard for me to strike that apprehensive tone. My low voice along with my above-average height in Japan exudes an aura of no-nonsense, self-confidence. So as much as I wished to acquiesce and blend in, I was far from convincing as I made what must have sounded like my half-hearted apologies for having a job.

By the time everyone gathered in the auditorium, the room was humming with the small talk of mothers sussing each other out. There was one notably, relaxed group—the women who already had older children at the school. They sat in the front row, emboldened with a been-there-done-that air, and chatted away until a teacher chastised, "Could you quiet down please?"

I was so impressed and envious that they were bold enough to weather a scolding.

•

Lest we be too happy about getting here, the principal urged us not to forget the families that had not been so fortunate. The acceptance rate had been about one in eight. "Please remember that there were many people to whom we could not offer a spot," he said. "Please work as hard as they would have." No congratulations or pats on the back for all that cramming and heartache. It struck me as a surprisingly stoic greeting, but I would later learn that these were The School's values at work. We were regarded as ambassadors of the proud institution and should not display undignified, giddy behavior. And past achievements are never good enough. There will always be more learning to do. This was the start of our humbling primary school experience where both mother and child would constantly be reminded of our deficiencies.

And then came the papers. At that first parents meeting, we were handed a stack of printed materials with detailed instruction on everything from where to write a child's name on the indoor sneakers (vertically, front-center, and also down the middle of the heel) to how to read the school's quadruple-colored Excel calendar. Throughout elementary school, reams of documents would fill our apartment, and every day I would sort and file them to keep abreast of school events, student goals, and parental duties.

There were about a dozen recurring newsletters and brochures covering topics ranging from the latest library book to glorious feats of the alumni. *School and Family* was sent out at the end of every semester and reported on each grade's accomplishments. It also offered guidance on how to spend the break between terms with solemn advice like this one on cell phones: "*If you are giving them [a cell phone], we hope you will also provide them with the right outlook (obligations and responsibilities).*" The teachers wrote monthly newsletters for each grade, explaining the curriculum and goals as well as reminders of major events like the all-school sports day and what items to bring from home for them. There was also a frequent, often daily, newsletter just for the class from each of the four homeroom teachers filled with musings from the teacher and reprints of student compositions.

I learned the ambitious philosophy behind all of these directives one day in a paper handed out during a parent-teacher
conference when Taro was in the second grade. A section titled
"We want to raise a child like this," listed the following four
profiles, all of which should be cultivated: "a child who can ini-
tiate a greeting," "a child who can communicate honestly with
and get along well with friends," "a child who can handle one's
responsibilities with care," and "a child who strives to find happiness in 'comprehension, capability and living life.'"

Health News was a monthly communiqué on wellness issues
such as how to avoid dehydration, precautions against food poi-
soning, information on prevalent infectious diseases, and basic
first aid. The School liked healthy, hearty children, and most of
the students were so. Several kids in Taro's grade did not miss a
single day of school for the entire six years of elementary school.
Only one child in his entire grade was overweight. The health
newsletter encouraged parents and children to be aware and
pro-active. It contained data like a bar graph illustrating the
number of flu cases by grade or the height and weight of The
School kids compared to the national average. The school monitored the health of children closely. There was an annual physical
and dental exam at school that included an electrocardiogram.
Mori Sensei checked his students' temperatures every morning by what he claimed was his failsafe hand-on-the-forehead
method. Somewhere along the line, he told us parents later, the
children started a practice where they would each make the fun-
niest face possible, wrinkling their noses and sticking out their
tongues as they stuck their foreheads out for inspection.

The monthly *Lunch News* listed the menu of the hot meal
served every day. Lunch was a serious business at The School,

prepared by staff in the kitchen onsite every morning and served on chinaware. The newsletter reported on the nutritional value of the ingredients and where they came from. It also described the fruits and vegetables in season, their health benefits and offered sample recipes for parents and kids to follow up on at home. Lunch consisted of a hot entrée, a vegetable, and dessert, which was usually fruit. Here is the menu entry for an average day:

Five-grain rice, hamburger with demi-glaze sauce, fresh salad, fruit, and milk. Foods for building bones, the body, and blood (beef, ground pork, eggs, milk); foods for energy and strength (rice, breadcrumbs, butter, olive oil, sugar); foods to help overall condition (onion, mushroom, cucumber, lettuce, pumpkin, carrots, raisins, lemon, fruits). The names of the producing farmers were then listed, along with the message: *"Let's understand the importance of food and not have leftovers."*

That last line was more of a command than a suggestion. The children were expected to finish everything served on their plate unless they had allergies. I once observed a girl and her teacher sitting across from each other at a table with a half-full plate of buttered carrots before the tearful student. The teacher, her chin resting on propped-up elbows, sat staring at the girl who slowly forced spoonfuls of the vegetable down while gagging and crying. Neither was going anywhere until the plate was empty. Fortunately, I never had any eating issues with Taro. He had no allergies and liked anything other than boiled shrimp, eggplant, green peppers, and mushrooms. Even as a toddler, he would gaze at plastic models of food displayed in Tokyo's restaurant windows, savoring what each dish might taste like.

July 4, 2006

Right now, I am in a panic. Three kids from First Grade Class South are having seconds on pineapple. I really like pineapple. I definitely want seconds. That's why I am in a panic and eating fast. When I look back I see that other people are still eating calmly. I haven't told anyone yet. That is because if there is only one pineapple, there won't be enough. Unfortunately, there was no seconds. But I did finish first.

Once a year, parents were invited to taste a meal and listen to a lecture by the school nutritionist.

"We chop forty kilos of cabbage," she proudly told us one year, explaining that she and the staff made daily eight-hundred meals for students and teachers, and that everything was done by hand rather than with the use of a food processor.

"A machine would scatter the water and dilute the taste," the nutritionist said. She urged us to uphold this practice of *tezukuri*, or handmade, at home and said that each child should be able to name a favorite mother's dish.

"Curry rice," I overheard Taro telling his friends. "My mom takes a block from the refrigerator and heats it in a pan."

No, no, no! I wanted to interject. I always made curry from scratch, sautéing onions, spices, and other vegetables and later adding chicken and curry powder. Taro had just seen me taking out a leftover frozen batch. But I did use a food processor to chop the vegetables.

The most frequent correspondences from the school were the reminders on what to bring. On the first day back after summer vacation, for example, the children should have: indoor uniform, indoor shoes, cotton gloves for weeding the campus grounds, and a towel to wipe away sweat. The indoor outfits, which the children changed into when they got to school, were dark-blue shorts and polo shirts of designated colors (white, yellow or pale blue) with name and class written on a white tag sewn on the upper-left side of the chest. Another day we were asked to provide dust cloths for the children to wipe their desks and lockers. Although janitors did thorough cleanings, students tidied up and swept the classrooms at the end of every day. That notice had a diagram of the preferred five-centimeter-wide cloth with a loop to hang on a hook, the child's name written on the bottom-left corner, and stitches running diagonally across in an X for durability. I'm a rusty seamstress, having barely held a needle since home economics class at my Japanese elementary school before moving to the US. The other mothers tailored these easily as they had honed their skills throughout their school years and cherished the art as housewives. I felt I should not cut corners and painstakingly hand-stitched Taro's first duster from an old washcloth. But later I discovered they sold fluffy white ones with all the required features at the local Walmart, so I just bought them there from then on.

When the school pool opened in June, we received a notice for the children to bring a swimsuit, a swim cap, a towel, and a plastic bag, all to be placed inside a designated yellow shoulder bag. Nails should be trimmed, ears cleaned, and the children should get a good night's sleep. We also had to take the child's temperature in the morning and record it in a chart to bring to school. I could have easily cheated and put down any number in the vicinity of 36.8 degrees centigrade, but I didn't want to suggest to Taro that it was OK to lie. So during breakfast on pool days I'd give him a quick poke with the ear thermometer.

For the first-grade school outing, a picnic at a local park, the packing list sent to parents contained seven items such as lunch, water canteen, picnic sheet, garbage bag, and tissues. By the fifth grade such inventories swelled to forty-three items for a five-night retreat, including, in addition to clothes and books, things like laundry pegs and bug spray. Instructions for overnight trips were always several pages long, with room assignments, hourly schedules, menus, and maps. I allotted a narrow table in our apartment hallway for Taro's *mochimono*, or gear. It was always piled high with clothes, books, folders, notebooks, and various unfinished projects arranged by the day they would be taken to school. Every day I crosschecked Taro's *mochimono* against lists from school.

Actually, Taro was supposed to be doing this himself. As soon as school started, the teachers steered the children toward independence, saying they should take care of their *minomawari*, which literally means one's immediate surroundings and usually refers to belongings. At the end of each school day the class leaders, elected by the students every semester, wrote on the blackboard the items that should be brought the following day, and the children copied the list into their notebooks. I admired this goal of self-sufficiency but prepared Taro's gear for him each day anyway because I knew that otherwise he would leave things behind and be reprimanded. The teachers kept track of the number of times a child forgot anything with consequences for the absent-minded like writing a self-criticism composition. "*I often cause trouble for other people because I forget things. I can't say it will never happen again. I am grateful to the people who lent me things when I forgot them,"* Taro wrote in a punitive assignment in the fifth grade. On another occasion, he was instructed to go to the principal's office and reflect on his shortcomings while sitting on the floor in the formal *seiza* style; back straight, knees together with legs folded under the body and hands on lap. For Taro, these punishments never served as the deterrent they were supposed to be. He just endured them as temporary discomforts that he simply needed to wait out.

Equally frowned upon was leaving anything behind at school, no matter how insignificant the item might seem. Twice a year, the school published a list of objects in the lost-and-found that would be laid out on a table for retrieval. The articles ranged from the run-of-the-mill sweaters and book bags down to tiny items like erasers and even hair-tying elastic bands. The point being that it was not the value of the item lost but the careless act that was the issue. To ensure that we parents were held under the same standards and setting a good example for the children, there was a separate list titled "Believed to belong to parents." It included items like cigarette lighters, jewelry, and even magazines. Picking up things from that table signaled that you or your child had been forgetful, not properly marking belongings with your child's name, and not handling possessions with appropriate care. I was generally good about inscribing Taro's name but one year had to claim a single chopstick that had been too small to mark. So keen to blend in, I didn't dare leave it there. It might have gone unnoticed, but I would have been exposed if anyone spotted Taro with the other matching chopstick. Another year, I endured a walk of shame with six umbrellas dangling on my arms. They all had Taro's name on them, but he had left them at school on days when the rain let up in the afternoon and kept taking new ones to school on rainy mornings.

•

Most children, like Taro, couldn't keep track of all the instructions, so we mothers diligently read the handouts and made sure our kids were properly armed. Sometimes the information was overwhelming even for me, though, and I once found myself scolded for not following directions properly. The handout from school before the first grade's potato-roasting festival—an annual event where the children cook potatoes in a fire pit—requested the students to bring an item to roast along with condiments. It explained that the potatoes would be wrapped in damp newspaper and aluminum foil. I had understood this to mean Taro should bring a potato and, separately, some foil and newspaper. But it turned out we were supposed to have prepared the entire package ahead of time. The next newsletter from Mori Sensei lamented that an extra twenty minutes was taken up to help the ten children who had not prepared their potatoes properly. "The children were scolded, but on balance, it seems there are problems with the attitude of the parents," he wrote. The following year, when I was all set to follow any instructions to a T, Mori Sensei's newsletter said, "Please refer to last year's instructions." So now I knew we were expected to save each and every directive ever brought home.

December 5, 2006

I went into the smoke. I put a pinecone, leaves, and about three branches into the fire. Now I am looking for a good place to roast my potato. The place where they bake to a good taste is where the ashes are red and hot. When I was looking around, I found a place like that. I crouched down and put it in quickly. I thought, "How much longer until I can eat it?" about the sweet potato in the ashes that I couldn't see anymore.

Most teachers did not give out their email addresses, and the school discouraged parents from phoning the school. For communicating with the school, we were given a notebook with a plastic green cover on it called "the green record book." All correspondence was supposed to be written in the green book. Since I had felt wrongly accused in the potato preparation incident, I entered the following justification in the book and had Taro give it to Mori Sensei.

"I am very sorry that I inconvenienced everyone at the potato-roasting the other day with my lack of proper preparation. I had mistakenly interpreted the instructions to mean that we only needed to bring the items on the list and that the preparation would be done at school."

I was pleased with my respectfully contrite note and eagerly awaited the teacher to write back that he had, indeed, been unclear. I never received a reply. I later found out that most mothers avoided writing at all in the notebook because they didn't want to have a record of things that might reflect poorly on them or their children. Until I became aware of that, I followed the school's instructions faithfully, writing every concern in the booklet. The early pages of my green book are filled with comments like, "He has left his cap at school three times now. I will have a talk with him about keeping track of his things." According to the other mothers, such an entry would forever label Taro as forgetful because it would remain there for the six years of primary school. Indeed, when I eventually ran out of space and went to the school office to get a new book, I discovered there was no such thing. The School only installed new pages into your original book like in a passport so that all entries were permanent. I never heard of any other mothers getting new pages.

My confusion over how to handle the green notebook was evidence that after all of the years I had spent in Japan, I still hadn't mastered the complex nuances of the culture's unspoken rules. The School didn't *really* want to have parents writing questions and comments to the teachers. They just put the book out there as a formality. Like the other mothers said, entries, particularly ones that reflect poorly on a child, might come back to haunt you. The other parents all had notebooks full of empty pages.

While all of the instructions could feel overbearing, I came to see that the detailed inventories from school served important purposes. They taught the children (and mothers) how to be organized by following a checklist. They also spoke to the ultra-democratic nature of Japanese society by assuring that everyone would have more or less the same items. No one would stand out with an extra fancy weeding glove. The only room for showmanship, at least in the first grade, was in the realm of whether one brought plain butter or cheese whip as a condiment for the roasted potato. For school outings, there were rules on how much money could be spent on snacks. A torturous pleasure for Taro was eyeing the candy shelf at the store to see how to best spend the one-hundred yen limit (about ninety cents).

In order to stay on top of all of the school requirements and to spend more time with Taro, who now came home in the mid-afternoon as opposed to the longer hours he had spent at day care, I quit my job at the resort and began doing freelance writing, mostly English-language columns about life in Japan, and translation of documents from Japanese into English. I was fortunate to have the option of living on a much smaller income. I would have to economize, but I wouldn't be out on the streets because I had the safety net of my parents. My father was never pleased that I wasn't financially independent, but he would always support me should I need it. My parents are quick to express their disappointment with my actions, but there is never any question about our loyalty to each other as family. When I told them I planned to adopt a child, they opposed on grounds that I didn't have it in me to raise a stranger. No one in our extended family or among their close friends had adopted.

"Adoption is something Christians do," my father said, which reminded me of a book I read as a child about a happy family that keeps adopting children. I can't remember the title, but I'm pretty sure they were devout Christians. I concluded I would not be able to change their minds and went ahead to Kazakhstan to meet Taro. From there I sent a fax to my parents not only announcing the adoption but telling them I had given him an important family name. Whatever their true feelings, my parents immediately sent a fax back saying how much they looked forward to meeting him.

June 14, 2006

Last night I took a bath with my grandfather. I made a water pistol with my hands and aimed for his mouth. It went straight into his mouth. My grandfather said, "I give up." I said, "Grandpa, you can do it, too." Then it became a big battle between us. After that we both laughed a lot.

Rationally, it was not a difficult decision to leave my job. Taro would only be young and malleable once, and I didn't want to miss those years. And I could do more writing, which I considered my real profession. Emotionally, it was a scary step to remove myself from that outer world of business attire, meetings, presentations, travel as a high-status frequent flyer, and the constant checking of an overflowing email box. I handed over my office key and building security pass and was instantly transformed into a woman who must justify her existence. My response to "what do you do?" would now be *okasan shitemasu* or "I'm doing motherhood"—a socially acceptable reply in Japan that reveals a recognition of the amount of work that a full-time mother does. The flipside, of course, is that society has not encouraged women to work outside of this traditional role.

At any rate, the idea of keeping my job at the resort was becoming increasingly complicated. Around this time, I had come to see how much resentment there had been against me at the office. The American president of the resort had agreed to pay for any babysitting fees incurred when I took Taro with me on business trips. So when I couldn't arrange for childcare in Tokyo, I happily took him along. It was stressful logistically to haul around a three-year-old, especially since Taro always threw up on planes, a terrible disruption to the travel of colleagues seated nearby. Once I pulled up in a taxi to the resort holding my overnight and computer bags in one hand and a paper bag full of vomit in the other. A quick-thinking employee held open a hotel shopping bag and signaled for me to put the bag in there so the boss's assistant could avoid walking around with a foul-smelling sack. But traveling with Taro allowed me to enjoy the best of both worlds: seeing him at breakfast and late at night while working frenetically during the day. I don't remember how I learned, but I found out that the other Japanese women who worked alongside me, most of them childless, felt that paying for Taro's childcare on the road was an unreasonable use of corporate funds for private needs. No matter that the resort president felt my work was worth that extra cost. The others wished he would hire someone without the liabilities of a child. Once again, I had failed to notice the unspoken, in this case, enmity. I was relieved to have resigned before any outright confrontation.

•

While we mothers were getting our feet wet wading through all of the papers, the children, too, were groping their way around their new environment. The first hurdle was for them to simply get there. Japanese children have traditionally traveled to school by themselves, and the crime rate is low enough to still allow that practice. Most children attend public elementary schools that are in walking distance of their homes. The schools and parents arrange for the children who live near each other to travel in groups. The practice increases safety and also encourages friendships between children of different ages, across different grades. Private school students are more likely to be on their own as they come from all over, not being zoned to a particular school district.

When Taro was in the first grade, to get from our apartment at the time in Komagome in central Tokyo to The School, in the western part of the city, he had to take two trains and a bus for the door-to-door journey that was about ninety minutes one way. It was a long commute, although he wasn't the furthest away. A few children traveled nearly two hours. Most students rode one train and then took the ten-minute public bus ride from the train station to school. The School had a system of easing the first graders into their commutes. The first week, parents would take them all the way to their classroom and later pick them up there. The second week, we would accompany them up to the campus gate. The third week, we went only as far as the school's local train station, and by the end of the first month, the children should be doing the entire commute on their own. It took me much longer than four weeks before I felt comfortable letting Taro make his journey alone. He had just turned six and looked awfully small in the Prussian suit or in the summer uniform of a white dress shirt, dark shorts, and a white rolled-brim hat. His tininess was accentuated by the fact that I had purchased everything in large sizes for him to grow into. Taro's black *randoseru*, the country's traditional leather satchel for elementary school children, covered most of his back. He was simply adorable. But also vulnerable. At first, my biggest concern was whether Taro could remember the way. Until then, I had never allowed him to leave our front door by himself. Now, at age six, he would have to walk along several city streets to get from our apartment to the local train station, board a crowded train and transfer at Shinjuku—the world's busiest station, where more than 3.5 million commuters pass through each day. Unfortunately, knowing one route would not always be enough since trains could be delayed or canceled. In those cases, pertinent transfer instructions are listed on screens in the trains and announced, but six-year-olds can't digest such information. One morning, a signal malfunction slowed his train line to school. I was seeing Taro off at Shinjuku as I sometimes did to ease my anxiety and was able to put him on another train. Several of his classmates were late that day including one who proudly announced that he had walked along the tracks with other passengers.

Shortly after school started, I encountered a scene that ratcheted up my anxiety level exponentially. A train approaching the platform across from us at Shinjuku one morning blasted its horn and stopped midway into the station.

"Get away from me!" shouted a young woman just a few meters ahead on the platform. She was trying to break free from two men grabbing her to stop her from jumping onto the tracks. I quickly moved in front of Taro to block his view. The men succeeded, and we were spared the scene of a bloody suicide. I knew such *tobikomi* ("diving in") suicides took place, but didn't realize how frequent they were. There were around six-hundred a year when Taro was commuting, according to government statistics, nearly two a day. Now I had to add, "might see a suicide" to my list of worries.

One day Taro breathlessly reported to me that he had discovered a one-hundred-yen coin left in a pay phone at Shinjuku. When he approached a station official to hand it over, "a man in a pale-blue shirt shouted some very bad words at me, so I ran to platform four," he said. I surmised that Taro had witnessed an exchange between the official and a distraught person "in a pale-blue shirt," whom I was relieved did not do anything rash like strike Taro. I always marveled at the fact that the private school children, easily identifiable by their school uniforms and who usually take the same route and ride in the same compartment every day, hadn't given rise to a spate of kidnappings. But there could always be a first. Japan boasts one of the world's lowest crime rates, but it's not crime free. Shortly before Taro started commuting, a seven-year-old girl was abducted on her walk home from a local public school and later found dead in a road-side ditch in Nara prefecture, about two-hundred-and-thirty miles southwest of Tokyo. Many public schools distribute alarm buzzers to their students, who hang the Oreo-size contraptions around their necks or on their satchels. Taro's teachers banned cell phone usage except for its GPS function so that parents could track their child's location. The School also had a system where parents received a text alert when their children arrived to or departed from campus.

It was distressing, but I felt I had to teach Taro that not every grown-up could be trusted. I instructed him to approach only station employees for help. I explained that I could not write his name on the outside of his satchel because "someone bad" might call it out to lure him away. Taro had a cell phone as well as prepaid pay phone cards to use in emergencies. Those items were stashed away in a zippered compartment of the *ran-doseru*, and I cringed to imagine him squatting in the middle of a busy platform, textbooks and pencil case spread out on the ground around him as he dug his way through his satchel. I sometimes saw little children in school uniforms doing that, immersed in their innocent bubbles amid a sea of rushing commuters. Always looming was the fear of a large earthquake, predicted to surely strike Tokyo at some point. Such a disaster would stall all train lines, and even if Taro survived the initial calamity, he would likely be engulfed by the ensuing panic.

Oblivious to my unending concerns, Taro bounded out of our apartment each morning at 6:30 a.m., so proud in his new uniform, turning around to wave at me several times along the way as I followed him to the station on my bicycle. So exciting for him, this newfound freedom of walking alone in a big city. I was glad that in Tokyo, Taro could experience this soaring sense of freedom that most of his friends in America were deprived of since their parents, and in many cases local authorities, judged it unsafe to have them roam around on their own. When his train arrived, Taro eagerly looked around for any schoolmates onboard. Once together, the boys used the time to practice writing characters on foggy windows, play hand games, and exchange riddles.

November 25, 2005

The first train I ride every morning is the Yamanote Line.[6] I play chopsticks[7] with my mama there. Mama doesn't get on the train if my friends are there. Today, Arakawa-kun[8] wasn't on the train. When I tried to get on the Chuo Line where I always do, a

---

6 The Yamanote Line and the Chuo Line are major Tokyo rail lines. The Yamanote Line loops around the center of Tokyo, and the Chuo Line links downtown Tokyo and the western metropolitan area.

7 A hand game involving adding and subtracting using the fingers.

8 The boys at school referred to each other by their last names, their first names or both names followed by the honorific title of -*kun*. When both names are used together, the last name comes first.

grown-up was throwing up. So I went a little bit further. Then I
saw Saito-kun on the Chuo line. We took my hat and played guess
which hand it's in.

A few months after Taro started school, as I was heading home from Shinjuku after seeing Taro off there, my train
pulled into a station where half an hour earlier a man had
thrown himself into an oncoming car. The corpse lay wrapped
in a sheet on a stretcher at one end of the platform. I scanned
the station to see if there were any helpless school children,
any white-rolled brim hats, among the crowd. There were not.
But I was sick of worrying twice a day, every day, about Taro's
commute and made the decision to move closer to the school.

•

Learning Tokyo's transportation system was just one of the
many challenges Taro encountered in his first year. There were
the initial power struggles among the children as they sized
each other up. On the one hand, these children had been raised
amid similar values. Their parents, or grandparents, like in our
case, were wealthy enough to afford the roughly ten-thousand
dollars of annual school fees and eager to spend that money
on a rigorous education. On the other hand, the kids were
already stressed from training intensely for several years for the
exams. Exhausted from all the memorization and drilling and
then praised for clinching a spot in a top school, now they
found themselves one among more than a hundred such little
stars. Like many children, Taro didn't tell me much about what
went on at school, but he did mention that during the first

few weeks many kids called him *gaijin* or foreigner because of his fair complexion and brown hair. (There was only one other non-Japanese student in Taro's grade: a girl with a Japanese mother and American father.) Not wanting to rub in the ugly fact that a foreign-looking boy is destined to be labeled a *gaijin* forever in Japan, I didn't respond to Taro beyond an acknowledgment of his report to me. He seemed to accept the epithet as a fact of life. To avoid one particularly rough boy, Taro told me that when he traveled from one classroom to the next he ran from pillar to pillar, taking cover to avoid being pummeled by the bully boy. Following The School's philosophy of fostering independent social skills, the teachers encouraged the children to sort things out among themselves and asked parents to stand aside as well. We were requested to contact the teachers rather than each other if we had concerns. The School didn't want sparks flying between angry mothers. My heart ached when I pictured my little boy crouching behind a pillar, but Taro didn't seem distressed so I didn't take any action. The boys did eventually reach a truce and even became friendly, although the bad boy later transferred to another school after his mother decided she didn't agree with some of The School's policies.

December 21, 2005

A long time ago I had many fights with Akiyama-kun. I thought "How come?" when he wouldn't let me play dodgeball. We became friends in music. We had fun talking when we were partners. When I hurt my leg he joked and said, "Are you doing alright there?" That was funny. I laughed. I don't like him. I don't like him. I don't like him. I like him. I like him. I like him.

One afternoon when Taro was walking down the long stretch from The School to the bus stop, a few kids took his cap and started tossing it back and forth when it got caught in a tree. The culprits saw Mori Sensei approaching, and a precocious girl among them quickly ordered the others to empty their wallets and handed the contents to Taro, asking him not to tell on them in exchange for the money. Mori Sensei scolded them all, including Taro, who was caught with a heap of coins in his hands. Sometimes the boys tussled, rolling around on the ground and hitting each other. As long as there wasn't any danger of physical injury, the teachers let such fighting go on. As a parent of an only child who has no siblings to wrestle with, I appreciated that leeway. I wanted Taro to get a sense of his strength and to learn sensible limits. That said, I always told him not to resort to physical force.

"If someone hits you, and you hit him back, you're just as bad as he is," I would say. "But if you don't hit him back, you're better than him."

But Taro didn't see it that way. "If you don't hit someone back, you're just stupid," was his retort.

Mori Sensei organized a wonderful game to calm those early tensions. He had the children divide into small groups and write down on tiny pieces of paper the traits they liked about each other such as "kind" or "funny." The children would then tape onto their clothes all of the compliments they had received. Each group took turns coming to the front of the class where they would act out the climactic scene of a popular TV drama in which a samurai, who parades around as a pauper, reveals his true identity and announces the virtues of someone he has rescued. In the classroom, the child in the samurai role would point to another child and read out loud the virtues pasted all over that child's body. The game had the kids laughing out loud at their silly acting while reinforcing the positive characters of each student.

Mori Sensei explained to the parents that he emphasized this game in particular because of the pressing need at the time to "have children know that they are loved." While the children were playing with their compliment cards, a strange, disturbing phenomenon had been unfolding around the country in which students appeared to be mailing anonymous suicide threats to the education ministry. The letter writers said they had been bullied, and that no one was taking their protests seriously. The Minister of Education released a statement urging parents to communicate openly with their children and saying, "Bullied children also have their pride, and it is said that they cannot easily disclose to their parents the facts of bullying." Fear gripped the country on November 11, 2006, the day on which some had declared they would carry out their suicide plans. On that day, The School locked its buildings and made sure access to higher floors was blocked. No students ended up taking their lives that day. It's hard to say whether bullying is on the rise in Japan or more prevalent than in other countries because of the subjective nature of what constitutes the act and because it's likely that many cases are not reported. But the issue is serious enough to be a frequently discussed topic. And school bullying often reflects some of the harsher aspects of Japanese culture such as the pressure to conform that discourages people from speaking out for, rescuing, or even just befriending a bullied classmate. I never sensed that bullying was a widespread problem at The School, at least not in Taro's class.

The School was part of a sprawling green campus that included a junior high, a high school, and a university. The children grew vegetables there, swam in a heated pool, and enjoyed well-equipped science, art, and music facilities. The School also had a retreat facility in a beautiful lakeside resort area about fifty miles southwest of Tokyo. A few months after they began school, the first graders took a two-night trip there. I have a photo of Mori Sensei and his twenty-eight pupils lined up naked in the large bath. (It's common for family members to bathe together in Japan through elementary school. The School kids and teachers all bathed together at retreats through second grade, and they separated by gender thereafter.) Taro is standing up, beaming and completely oblivious to his showing full frontal. One mother told me she was saving the photo in case Taro becomes famous one day.

Everything was new and exciting during those early years. Taro was in a top school. I was digesting all of the directives and following instructions, adjusting to my new status as "a mother." (Or at least a more full-time one.) We moved to an apartment close to The School. Taro was thrilled with each new step. We were full of hope.

July 5, 2006

We got a lot of American cherries from my grandmother's friend. If I swallow it with the pits, a cherry tree might grow from inside my stomach. What would that be like? I would still want to be the normal me. At school, in the bath, I will be with the cherry tree. Flowers will grow, and birds will poke me. I would say, "Stop that!"

III

Overloaded

June 6, 2006

• • •

IT'S A TUESDAY, SO I LAY OUT TARO'S SOCCER JERSEY, SHORTS, and socks in the entryway. "Hurry, hurry, hurry," I greet him at the door mid-afternoon and practically strip off his school uniform and help him into his athletic wear. He hands me his satchel, and I give him a knapsack with his soccer ball in it. No time to sit down for a snack, so I throw a piece of candy into his mouth. We have our own special word for this feeding action; *nageire*, which literally means "throwing in," but is actually a technical term in the art of flower arrangement where cuttings are arranged in a natural, free style. We grab our bikes from the apartment's basement garage and ride twenty minutes to the field.

"Stop zigzagging," I shout as I tailgate him on the path through a park. "Each loop like that takes up more time."

Like the majority of Japanese families, we were swept up in lesson mania. By enrolling Taro in various after-school classes, I was hoping he would learn to swim and compute as well as the other kids, and that I might even stumble across a talent to mine. In the second grade, he had six different after-school classes. On Monday he had abacus; on Tuesday and Thursday he had soccer and abacus; on Wednesday he had piano; on Friday he had swimming and abacus; and on Saturday he had English and judo.

It was a fairly orthodox selection. Eighty percent of Japanese elementary school students take after-school classes. The classes aren't cheap. I was spending around four-hundred dollars a month on them. Such costs have a serious repercussion on society. Japanese women have among the fewest children in the world, one or two on average, and they often say the high cost of raising a child holds them back from having more.[9] The majority of Taro's classmates had no siblings, and when they approached their late teens in 2015 Japan's population recorded its first official decline since the census was begun in 1920.[10]

"What classes does your child take?" was a common question among the mothers. We all wanted to make sure we weren't missing something that could leave our kids on the bottom rungs. Most of the children in Taro's grade took swimming lessons, in part to make sure they would perform well in the annual school tournament. Every fall, the four classes of each grade competed against each other before cheering parents in a variety of relays. At the first-grade meet, nearly all of the children could swim the length of the twenty-five-meter pool. And while everyone cheered politely, you didn't want to end up like Mrs. Kimura, whose son held our class team back. He managed the length but with several stops to stand and wipe his

9 http://www.mhlw.go.jp/wp/hakusyo/kousei/13/dl/1-02-3.pdf, 97 (Japanese)

10 http://www.stat.go.jp/english/info/news/20160420.htm

face. The mothers offered a subdued clap while Mrs. Kimura repeatedly bowed her head slightly with an exaggerated furrowed brow as she said "*sumimasen*," sorry, to those around her.

These extracurricular classes came after a full day of school, so exhaustion was a frequent topic at parents' meetings. Concerns included grogginess and the mixing up of various lesson bags. Many children went straight from school to these classes, so they had to bring their swimming or abacus bags with them in the morning with plenty of chances of leaving them on the train or bus along the way or mixing them up with someone else's.

March 14, 2006

Today I went to abacus. I did drills with two rows. You must concentrate to do it quickly. After I move the beads, I space out so I don't know which part I am doing any more. Right now I am thinking that I am stupid.

When I was in the second grade, after-school classes were rare in Japan. So after I dropped my book satchel off in our entryway, I headed out to play until dark. I remember roller-skating around our apartment complex and daydreaming away the afternoons on the swing set in the communal playground. Taro and his classmates enjoyed little if any downtime. If Taro let his mind wander even momentarily during abacus, the teacher would shout, "Focus!" When he leaned against the goalpost during a soccer match once, aimlessly watching the clouds go by, some dad (fathers came to weekend games) yelled, "What's the matter with that goalie?"

I was aghast. I didn't think about how tired Taro must have been, or about how nice it was to see a child engrossed in minute of fantasy. I was thinking how ashamed I would be if the ball went into the goal. I should have lessened the burden for Taro, but at the time everything seemed indispensable. Taro enjoyed soccer, and I felt it might be the only period in his life when he could feel exhilarated by a sport that he wasn't a star in. And wasn't it good to foster a team spirit? Abacus should cure his slow pace of addition and subtraction and improve his concentration. Piano opens up the world of music appreciation, and English opens up the world itself. Swimming was a must for the school meets as well as a survival skill. I hoped that judo would instill a Bushido spirit into a boy deprived of male kinship after his father had stopped communicating with us around the time Taro started school.

The extra-curricular classes were also a chance to make friends outside of school, many from our new neighborhood, and to socialize in a more diverse circle than that of his privileged classmates. I could rationalize ad nauseam, but I can't deny that I also just wanted to keep up with everyone else. Once in a while, Taro said things that jolted me awake to the reality of his overscheduling. "The sooner you get there, the sooner you can . . ." I was saying one evening, trying to come up with an enticement to rush him to his next activity. Huffing and running alongside me in the frigid winter air, abacus beads jiggling in his knapsack and hair still wet from swimming, Taro smiled and finished the sentence for me. ". . . have time for a walk outside?"

And, of course, there was also school. Here, Taro's second-grade classes included art, Japanese, math, physical education, integrated studies,[11] music, and English.

Like all Japanese primary schools, The School used a selection of government-approved textbooks. But the teachers augmented studies with the school's own, more advanced study materials. In many subjects The School taught concepts beyond the standard guidelines for that grade, and it prided itself on not having followed a government policy in the 1980s that reduced curricula and class hours. Amid this rigorous academic program, Taro faltered from the start. After observing him unable to answer a lot of questions in class during a parental visit event, I worried that he wasn't absorbing the material as quickly as the other children. I told Mori Sensei several times about my concerns but only got half-hearted replies that he would keep an eye on Taro. I asked one mother who had an older boy at the school whether any remedial instruction was offered.

"Oh no," she replied. "This is a private school, and the teachers cater to the higher-level students."

Since parents had groomed their children upward and were paying expensive tuition, they didn't want school standards to decline by slowing the pace to help struggling students keep up. And The School expected me, not the teacher, to keep Taro up to speed. Toward the end of second grade, I asked Mori Sensei if Taro should be tested for learning disabilities, just in case I was pushing him to do something he really couldn't do.

---

11 Integrated studies was an interdisciplinary subject at The School which in younger years focused on observations of nature and growing vegetables. In the later years, it was similar to home economics.

"He just barely does not have one," came the reply, which was slightly puzzling to me. Don't you either have or not have a learning disability? But Mori Sensei's answer catered to my wishful thinking that Taro had no serious impediments and dissuaded me for the time being from further investigation.

I fantasized about Taro rising up above his classmates in every subject. I felt such accomplishments would reflect my strengths as a mother. Or maybe I was looking to compensate for my own lack of achievements. For as long as I can remember, my mother urged me to look up to my father and brother, both of whom had excelled at school and graduated from Harvard, effectively telling me I was nothing when measured against them.

"You should marry someone just like Daddy, or if that doesn't work, someone like Jun," she would say. My brother was valedictorian both in primary school and high school. I was mostly a B student.

"Isn't it great that the *boy* is the one who does better," she'd say. "Think about how awful it would be if the girl was the smarter one." I suppose my mother was trying to comfort me for being perennially average. The only thing I remember being told I did better than Jun was getting invited to birthday parties. But even then, my mother skewed the results in his favor: "It's amazing that Jun doesn't get upset when you get all the invitations."

My life continued in Jun's shadow. My brother had a successful career as a banker in the US and Japan and is happily married (to another Harvard grad) with two high-achieving sons. The stars of admiration for my brother and father forcibly etched into my pupils affected my relationships with men. Every boyfriend I had was held up to the intimidating standards of my brother and father. During the prime dating years of my late twenties, my brother was on track to become a partner at a major investment bank, and my father was a candidate for the presidency of Japan's largest trading company. They didn't get there with a lack of self-assurance and had no sympathy for nervous suitors. Ironically, this turned out to be a big plus in the column of my brash ex-husband whom I met when we were both reporting for American news magazines and covering the funeral events for Emperor Shōwa in Tokyo.

"He's smarter than the other ones," my father noted after listening to him pontificate over dinner about Japanese trade practices.

My mother added, "I wonder what he sees in you." That actually turned out to be a good question. If I had asked myself that instead of marveling at his talents and confidence, I might have been more vigilant and noticed that he had a girlfriend in another city when we married and been spared the heartache of a twelve-year marriage to a man with so many secrets.

"I should have hired a private detective to check up on his past," my mother still likes to say nearly thirty years later, reminding me of my poor judgment. I wanted Taro to lift me above them all, to remove that boulder off my shoulder.

•

While I fretted about his performance, Taro seemed happy and carefree. By the second grade, we had moved to an apartment that was a walk and bus ride from campus—about a thirty-minute commute in all. He relished the unsupervised journey to school, kicking stones and collecting insects en route.

September 4, 2007

"Oh!" I found a cicada. It was lying down by the entrance to the restaurant. It's alive but on its back and cannot move. I put out my thumb, and when it stuck, I lifted it up. The cicada quickly flew away. It went above the buildings, and then I couldn't see it anymore.

After I walked a little, I heard a rustling noise in the grass. I put both hands in there and knew it was a cicada. It's moving like it crashed and is confused. I tried to fly it, but it crashed to the ground and cannot fly well. When I did it again, it flew up to the buildings and then disappeared into the clouds where I couldn't see.

Today at The School I took one from the corridor and put it in a dented part of a tree root. After that, I put some leaves on it. When I looked on my way home, it was gone.

I am glad I saved three of them.

Taro still left home early so he could join in what the kids called *mon machi*, or "gate waiting" which referred to arriving before the school entrance opened at 7:30 a.m. (Students had to be at their desks by 8:25 a.m.) Once allowed in, the children rushed to their classrooms, changed into their in-school uniforms, and ran outside to play until the first bell. For Taro, school revolved around the short recesses: three of them in the morning and two in the afternoon. Every chance he got, Taro was outside playing soccer, softball, and dodgeball, or building forts. After school ended in mid-afternoon, the kids changed back into their official, more formal dress and jammed into the public bus that had a stop near the campus entrance and ended at the local train station. The high noise level and unwieldy satchels banging about were the source of ceaseless complaints from other riders.

Taro savored every minute of the walk from the station to our home. Sauntering along, his white dress shirt sloppily hanging out of the waistline of his dark-blue shorts, he peered into shops, pushed the buttons on vending machines, and scoured the grounds for treasures.

October 20, 2006

Right now I am putting away a pinball token. It will be terrible if someone sees it and throws it away. Actually, I have been looking for things from before that could be treasures. I found a nail, an orange thing from a bike, and something you play a guitar with. I want to keep finding things and open a shop. I'll try hard.

After I complained to him about the accumulating junk in his room, my mother found him hoarding items in a small cluster under some bushes near our apartment.

"Just like a crow," she said.

Sometimes Taro went inside shops on his way home from school. Once he was so hungry he picked up a piece of deep-fry batter that had dropped onto a ledge beneath a deli counter and savored it in his mouth as he ran out exhilarated with his "shop-lifting," as he later put it to me. When he finally arrived home, I'd be there with his lesson bags, fuming because he was late.

The academic year that started in April and ended in March revolved around a number of annual school events, many of which the children spent weeks preparing for. Sports Day was held in May. "There's nothing as fun as this," Taro told me one year. In addition to the standard relays and obstacle courses, the first graders ran a race holding a ball while balancing a sand-filled bag on their heads while the fifth graders played a rough game called "cavalry battle" where a child hoisted up by three others tries to topple over another child in the same position with pushing and shoving. In October, students displayed academic reports and artwork and performed plays at the school fair. There was the potato-roasting festival in December and later that month the school concert where each grade performed a number of songs, both vocally and with instruments. At the February race, called "the marathon," the children ran one or two kilometers around campus.

Like many of the activities, the marathon encouraged competition. A teacher called out the ranking of each runner crossing the finish line as mothers lined up by the goal and cheered and clapped. Sometimes the last child in, followed by a teacher on a bicycle, would be in tears. Each year Taro and I agreed on a list of prizes and punishments for his performance. The rewards served to motivate, and the fear of penalties added a layer of thrill to our contract. There were twenty-six children in the second grade so that year, we drew up a list of twenty-six items. First place was a visit to Disneyland. I knew he would never get this one, so I let it be extravagant. Third place won a trip to the movies, seventh place was ice cream, and for tenth place I would make him a full hot breakfast as opposed to our usual yogurt and toast. From the mid-point, thirteenth place and down, were punishments beginning with a haircut done by me. (Taro preferred the barbershop over my bowl cut.) Nineteenth place required that he write an extra diary entry, twenty-first place was an hour of piano practice, and for the last, twenty-sixth place, eight pages of *kanji*[12] writing. Taro always raced hard but came in among the slower half of the class: in punishment territory.

———————————

January 31, 2007

Bang. The starting sound surprised me, and I was late starting. I chased after everyone in a panic. It's hard to catch up. There are about 20 people ahead of me, so it's a big deal to go around them. "Shoot." I was getting mad.

At the West Gate, I remembered the way the fast runner Mizu-kami-kun runs. He makes his posture a little bit low. Oh, I passed three people. It feels like, "Not bad." Kiyoshi-kun who is in front of me, knows I am behind him and increased his pace. Next I remembered how my cousin told me to run with big steps and tried that. I passed Kiyoshi-kun, and I wasn't even tired. I did my final sprint from the elementary and junior high school sign. I was 21st. The punishment my mother and I agreed on is piano practice for one hour. The punishment for 22nd place is four pages of kanji, *so I am glad I did not get that one.*

———————————

Every year, each grade went on two separate day trips and one sleepaway retreat. The lengths of the retreats varied from two nights for the first graders to one week for the sixth graders. The excursions for the older pupils took on stronger academic

---

12 *Kanji* are the Chinese characters that are used as part of the Japanese written language. Primary school children learn 1,006 of them over the course of six years.

characteristics as well as measures to encourage independence. Where the first-grade trip might be to a park, the sixth graders would study temples. For the day trips, the older children were expected to get to the destination by themselves on public transportation. All the trips included activities to toughen character, like strenuous hikes. A freak hailstorm struck Taro's first grade trek, sending icy stones the size of golf balls down onto the children as they ate lunch on the mountaintop before making their descent. One activity during the third-grade trip was a *kimodameshi*, literally a testing of the gut, and a traditional summer spook custom in Japan, originating from the idea that being frightened enough to get the chills cools one off in the summer heat. At the gut test, the teachers told the children ghost stories and made them walk to isolated destinations at night in the dark. Some kids laughed, and some kids cried. After each event, the children had to write compositions about them. Here's a report Taro wrote on the hailstorm in the mountains.

Right now I am lining up by Jyofudai[13] and thinking about how far it is to Byobu Mountain.

After we left, my legs got tired when we passed the cedar trees. It was the first time I went hiking so I got really tired. But I tried hard. The more I try, the more tired I get. The more tired I get, the more hungry I get. But I am trying hard.

Finally, we reached the top. But as soon as we got there, it started thundering. Poor Takahashi-kun is plugging his ears. I'm trying hard to help him. I carried his knapsack for him.

"It's so heavy."

---

13 Jyofudai is the name of a large grassy area in front of the school retreat building in the countryside.

"Oh, sorry I made you carry it."
We talked like that.
I had a really hard time.

Taro was a perceptive and creative writer, but it was a feat to squeeze the words out of him. Unfortunately for me, anything not completed at school was brought home to be finished under my supervision. The amount of homework varied according to the teacher. Mori Sensei's policy was twenty minutes multiplied by the grade number. So in second grade, Taro should have been sitting at his desk after school for forty minutes. He managed maybe fifteen under my close supervision. On top of that, The School had a tradition of requiring all students to keep a diary with a minimum of three or four entries a week. To encourage him, my mother conjured up a cartoon of a boy called "Diary Boy" who feeds on diary entries. Pictures of Diary Boy, usually hungry, would mysteriously pop up in Taro's diary book when he slept over at his grandparents' or they would appear on postcards and letters in the mail.

June 23, 2007

A recent postcard is one from Salzburg with a picture of Mozart on it.
    I'm talking now about postcards from my grandmother. My grandmother has been to places like Austria, Australia, and Africa. My grandmother draws comics to try to get me to write my diary. But it doesn't work that well. I don't like to write my diary.

Maybe writing letters is like studying, too. I think my grandmother is great. She also prints my photos on the postcards. I get two letters every week. Once there was a stamp with a photo of my grandmother. I thought, "I wonder how they did that."

I want to ask my grandmother that. I am putting the letters in a file. I think soon that file is going to be full.

•

Our homework standoffs during those earlier years of elementary school began as soon as Taro got home from after-school activities. He would lie on his bed and pull out a book to read. That may sound promising, and I admit that his love of reading was wonderful. (And it was only sustained because I didn't buy him any electronic games.) But in the meantime, homework needed to be done. Taro never wrote down his assignments, so I would open his satchel and search through the crumpled papers to try to figure them out. If that didn't work, I called other mothers or his classmates.

Once I learned what the duties were, I'd lay the necessary papers out on our dining room table and next to them a plate of snacks to lure Taro over like a hungry little animal. He came over to eat but would quickly move to the sofa for more leisurely reading or to play with cards or marbles. I could usually coax him to return to the table and sit for a few minutes. But soon his mind would wander and he'd be back on the sofa or run off to his room. I would try to entice him back, dangling various carrots including candy or sometimes even cash. At one point, I had a whole chart system with daily and weekly goals and prizes. And lots of compliments on work completed, just as the parenting books tell you to do. But eventually, after several rounds of back and forth from bed to table to sofa to table, I would lose my temper.

"Just do it!" I'd shout. "Look how late it is now. Why can't you do it like the other kids?"

If Taro ran away from the table, I would chase after him and drag him back to his chair. If I pointed out mistakes or asked him to repeat something as a drill, he would glare at me, exposing the whites of his eyes and throw pencils and erasers around the room.

Our battle of wills could go on for hours, with the stakes rising as evening approached. When he consistently ignored my commands to put away his Pokémon cards, I would grab a few and threaten to tear them up or douse them in water in the sink. He usually still refused. So I would proceed, storming over to the kitchen sink and opening the tap, and finally throwing the cards under the running water. I spent many late nights hanging fading wet cards on a laundry line with clothespins and later ironing their curled-up corners. Some items ended up beyond repair like a small plastic case that I had filled with candy when we went on trips for as long as we could remember. We'd called it the sweetie box. In one fit of rage I had dangled my foot above it with the usual threat of "unless you start working right now . . ." Met with continued defiance, I stomped on the blue box that had accompanied us on so many holidays and crushed it. One night while I was yelling, I banged my fist down on his bookshelf. My little finger swelled up to the extent that I was worried it would not fit into my ski glove that weekend when we were planning to go on a trip with another school family. I sheepishly confessed to the mother, who laughed and told me, "Don't worry. I've done exactly the same."

I was obsessed with making Taro do all of his homework, and in these younger years, I would eventually succeed. We would both be exhausted, sometimes leaving a trail of smashed toys, but the assignments got done. And by bedtime all was peaceful. Taro still had unquestioning affection for me. I was still his world.

November 6, 2006

Right now, I am throwing a ball that my mother can catch. Actually, we are at Triangle Park inside Inokashira Park now playing catch. My mother returned a good one like mine. It was so much fun. I wanted to play again. Maybe she can throw a good one because we ate crepes before. The park was crowded because it was Sunday. The ball we used for catch is a real ball. We easily threw 100 times. Then we went to the bars. I practiced pullovers. I wanted to play catch at that park, too, but my mother said, "No."

•

Japanese elementary schools don't believe children should hang loose even during vacations, so we never got much of a break. Apart from when he was at sleepaway camp in the US, there were only a few days throughout the entire six years of elementary school that Taro did not do some sort of home-work. "*Unless you are vigilant, you could end up spending time passively,*" warned one *School and Family* newsletter before an extended holiday. It suggested, "*Do you want to organize your drill sheets and test papers?"* Teachers assign large amounts of homework over vacations to make sure students don't lose academic momentum. They also believe that keeping children busy thwarts delinquency.

At private schools, where there are more full-time mothers than at public schools, the mothers spent a lot of time overseeing their children's work. The nature of involvement varied, ranging from just making sure an assignment was completed, which was what I aimed for, to super coaching for prize-winning work. I knew one mother who guided her daughter during summer breaks to finish numerous independent projects that would be submitted in installments over the course of the school year like taking items from a stocked shelf. Her daughter used the extra time she earned that way during the school year to roar ahead academically or to focus on extracurricular activities. According to a 2016 Japanese government survey, nearly 40 percent of children between the ages of ten and fourteen are with their mothers when they do homework,[14] and a 2016 survey by the education and publishing firm Benesse showed more than 20 percent of parents "advised and worked together throughout" their children's summer projects and book reports.[15] Museums, parks, and major stores offer homework fairs every summer to help children with their "independent" research assignments. Bookstores set up special displays of how-to publications with titles like *Easy Independent Projects.* Such heavy-handed

14 https://www.e-stat.go.jp/stat-search/files?page=1&layout=datalist&toukei=00200533&tstat=000001095335&cycle=0&tclass1=000001095399&tclass2=000001095400&tclass3=000001095402&stat_infid=000031653782&second2=1 Excel, 20 (Japanese).

15 Benesse Holdings Newsletter, July 24, 2017 (Japanese).

instruction from all corners doesn't give children much opportunity to think on their own or play with ideas, which may be one of the reasons why in global comparative surveys by the Organization of Economic Cooperation and Development (OECD), Japanese students demonstrate good understanding of scientific facts and theories but show little confidence in their abilities to apply such information.[16]

Teachers at The School were resigned to the heavy parental hand.

"Please make sure the work includes some ideas or thoughts from your child," Taro's third-grade science teacher told us when explaining an assignment to invent a useful appliance.

No engineer myself, I turned for help to my cousin who is an architect. He already knew the drill, having once had to build a miniature Swiss pasture on a music box for the pre-school project of a client's granddaughter. The invention assignment was a summer homework tradition at The School in which children third grade and above must create something useful out of simple materials lying around the house. The gadgets were exhibited at school, and the best ones were entered into a Tokyo contest. Taro's classmate was honored one year for making a small, bean-filled cushion to put eggs on so they wouldn't roll around on a kitchen counter.

Every summer my cousin spent two days with us, patiently encouraging Taro to come up with some ideas and then guiding him through the construction. I was always sizzling with rage because while we two adults were wracking our brains, Taro was either throwing out unrealistic suggestions—"a pair of sunglasses

---

16 http://www.oecd.org/pisa/pisa-2015-Japan.pdf, 5

that fill in the scenery as you imagine it!"—or running off to his room to read comic books. The first year we made a perforated cardboard shoe that fit inside a sneaker and could be attached to a vacuum cleaner hose. It was supposed to suck dirt out from shoes. The next year, we took a clipboard and pasted on top of it a piece of thick cardboard with slots carved out to hold a pencil, ruler, and eraser. We fashioned a transparent plastic sheet on top of the cardboard that would slide from side to side, covering and uncovering the slots. The "clipboard pencil case" would be useful for note taking on field trips. The following year, feeling we didn't ace the competition because the clipboard had been too sophisticated, we downgraded to a "reminder sweatband" that was a wristband with Post-it notes stapled all over where you could write down your homework assignments. Our final year, we stuffed a fluffy cloth into a goggles case and claimed it was an eyeglass case that cleaned the lenses every time you pulled your glasses out. When Taro struggled to remove the glasses during his presentation, his classmates jeered that it would be much quicker to wipe the lenses by hand. We never got any honors. But years later I saw on a website a clipboard very similar to ours being marketed as a new product, and my cousin said we should have registered for a patent.

On a ten-day Christmas holiday to Hawaii, when Taro was in the third grade, he had to complete five pages of math, four pages of writing practice, three pages of reading comprehension, two geography quizzes, two independent reports, an English alphabet sheet, a book log, the diary, and an ancient Japanese card game.

Apart from a special furlough for Christmas day, I doled out daily quotas for Taro. I had gotten my Master's degree at the University of Hawaii, and I called on my old colleagues for help. One afternoon I took Taro to the East-West Center where I had worked as a student and knew the president. I left Taro in the president's office, hoping that the presence of a stranger would intimidate him into writing that day's quota of twenty sentences using newly learned Chinese characters. I used that time to walk around the university campus to search for independent report topics. I found a sausage tree bearing giant sausage-shaped fruit. Perfect. I called my ex-boyfriend from graduate school, a marine scientist, and asked him to take us to a museum where we humored Taro into copying an illustration of a rabbit that also looks like a bird for a report on optical illusions. And late at night, the melodious voice of a former Japanese classmate reverberated down the hotel corridor as she chanted some of the one-hundred poems that Taro needed to memorize to master a thirteenth-century card game.

Of course, Taro didn't fulfill the quotas without putting up a struggle. One day while we were arguing over some assignment, he ran out of our Waikiki hotel room. By the time I opened the door a few seconds later, the long hallway was empty. In a mild panic, I called the room of a school friend's family who was staying at the hotel next door. To my relief, he was there.

"They're writing their diaries," the mother said. My comrade-in-arms.

December 26, 2007

(I'm really mad.) Those last words my mother said really made me mad. I dashed to my friend's heaven. I called the elevator, and unfortunately one family was in it. In America there is a law that kids cannot go out by themselves. I stood in the corner so people would not see me. I took a secret passage but got lost. But I want to take the shortcut before my mother catches up. But my mother was being slow, and it was getting creepy being by myself.

We were heading over to the dark side of the elementary school years.

May 10, 2007

I took out the red origami box from the treasure chest. If you put a pencil in the origami, the lead will leave a pencil mark.

My mother's treasure chest has all of the presents I gave her.

1. *Two bracelets. One is something they were handing out for free at a store. It has beads that look like tops and a silver chain. It is transparent so you can see your skin. The other one has an acorn in the middle and paper balls on elastic. There are pearls between the paper balls. I made it at day care.*

2. *Necklace. A lot of beads are on elastic. I made this at camp in America.*

3. *A rock. (A small stone.) It is a perfect round stone one centimeter diameter. I found it in the hallway of our building.*

4. *A doll. (Miniature) My day care teacher made it. It says Yataro on the bottom of its pants.*

The box has five things in it. I think my mother really likes them because they are all very useful. She can wear the jewelry when she is going out. The doll and stone, she can just look at, and they will remind her of me.

I am on the lookout for more useful things.

IV
The Mothers

July 20, 2007

* * *

I'M STANDING AT THE CAMPUS ENTRANCE MAKING SMALL TALK with a group of mothers from Taro's class. If I see Taro's homeroom teacher, I need to buttonhole him for chitchat. I try to seize every opportunity to strengthen my connection with him as a conduit to Taro's school world. But I need to do that subtly, so it doesn't look like I'm upstaging the other moms and trying to get cozy with the faculty. We are seeing the children off as they embark on their annual retreat. As the coach buses drive away, we wave until they're out of sight. Then we scatter into small groups. Today I don't have to anxiously tag alongside a random cluster of mothers because I've already secured an invitation to go for coffee with one of the cliques.

As Taro immersed himself into student life, I delved into the parallel world of the mothers. Warnings of the pitfalls in this society came early. A few months before Taro enrolled, I exchanged emails with a woman whose son had attended The School some years earlier. Among the various bits of advice she gave me was not to join the PTA until after I had a sense of what the other mothers were like.

"I had a terrible experience. I was bullied when I did PTA work when my son was in the first grade," she told me. Bullying among the moms? I didn't know the woman well enough to pry details out of her, but I suspected that she must have somehow stepped out of line in this conformist country. That would be easy for me to do, too, with my unconventional past. Taro had passed the entrance exams; now it was my turn to jump through hoops to pass muster with the moms.

•

"What's 'a mothers' lunch?'" an Australian friend asked me when I told her I couldn't meet her because of such an event. During the primary school years, I had gotten so used to the common reference for these ostensibly social gatherings that I had used it in conversation as if it were a routine business engagement. I did in fact treat the meals like work, in that I dutifully attended as many as I could and kept mental notes on the takeaways. The coffees and lunches among the mothers sometimes consisted of trivial chatting. But more often than not, they were also crucial opportunities to gather information and check on one's standing in The School's social circles. I went to my first mothers' lunch two weeks after Taro started school. Two PTA representative mothers from our class, who knew the ropes from having older children at the school already, arranged the gathering at a French restaurant near the campus. Like all lunches, it was held on a weekday. Even among the minority of mothers who worked, most seemed to have flexible enough jobs to allow them to come to these midday socials. The PTA-organized get-togethers took place only once or twice a semester, but smaller groups of mothers met informally a few times a month. When there was an event at school, like the swim meet or the marathon race, cliques of mothers would always go to lunch before or afterward.

March 28, 2008

Characteristics of grown-ups:

1. *They like numbers.*
2. *They write messy on purpose.*
3. *They are nervous.*

Nearly all of the twenty-eight mothers of First Grade Class South attended that first meal. The two veteran moms greeted us at the entrance to the private area upstairs of the bistro and collected money for the prix fixe course they had selected in advance. Then we picked numbers out of a paper bag and sat at places where there was a tiny piece of paper with the corresponding figure. Those detailed arrangements deterred spontaneity that could give rise to the slightest of awkward situations. You wouldn't want to be caught hesitating before sitting next to someone, for example, or ordering an appetizer when everyone else just had a main course. The degree of care that went into the scripting of social settings would surprise me throughout the school years. I was puzzled once when a mother asked me if we would be meeting somewhere beforehand to walk over to a lunch I had organized even though I had distributed the address, phone number, and website with a map to the restaurant. The location of the restaurant was clear enough, another mother explained to me, but no one wanted to show up first and be alone for even a few minutes. It would be preferable to meet at a train station or department store where arriving first would be less noticeable among the bustle of anonymous crowds.

At that first luncheon, we made small talk around two long, white-clothed tables while eating a French meal of three small-portioned and tasty enough courses. Once the table was cleared of all except the coffee, the organizers asked us to introduce ourselves. One by one the mothers stood up, identified themselves by their children's names, bowed, and said something self-effacing.

"I'm Yasuko Sekiguchi's mother," said a petite woman with black eyeliner drawn evenly around both eyes, demarking them perfectly against the backdrop of her porcelain complexion. "My recent worry is that I'm getting patches of bald spots from the stress of the entrance exams."

Another woman said she had put on so much weight during her son's entrance exam prep that she was following a yoga regime popular with celebrities to shed the pounds. A few introduced their own hobbies like skiing or making beaded flowers. All of them apologized for their children being unruly and incompetent, using terms like *baka* or stupid. "I'm very sorry that we might cause trouble," was a common closing remark.

"I'm Yataro Makihara's mother," I began. "We started late in the exam process, and I have always been busy with work," I said, lining up the excuses before the apology. "My son is rambunctious and doesn't listen to me, and I am very sorry that we will cause a lot of problems." Then I decided to add something that I thought might be a way of ingratiating myself with the group. I now regret it and am embarrassed to recall my naiveté. "I have lived overseas for a long time and can speak English," I said. "So if any of you ever need any help with English, please let me know. I would be very happy to be of any assistance." In the cultural context of Japan, where humility is valued, I might as well have announced my superiority. I found out later that many of the mothers had lived or studied abroad themselves. No one told me that at the lunch, though. Everyone just listened politely.

The typical mother of a child in Taro's first grade class was a college-educated woman in her late thirties who had worked until she got pregnant and then became a full-time mother and homemaker. Among the minority who continued to have jobs, a few were medical doctors, some had office administrative positions, and some were part-time teachers or tutors. I had just started my freelance writing and translating work. Nearly all of the women were married. Among the 112 mothers of Taro's grade, just four of us were divorced, one of whom later remarried. Fathers attended major school events like Sports Day and open classrooms, but mostly the mothers took charge of school-related affairs. With their similar profiles, the mothers even seemed physically alike to me.

I remember being struck by their sameness when I witnessed a bizarre scene at a PTA meeting. A dozen or so mothers had encircled a teacher and were bowing deeply. They were apologizing after being scolded for chatting too noisily at The School's Sports Day. Backs ramrod straight and waists bent at a ninety-degree angle, foundation-polished faces and dark hair, semi-expensive, tasteful if bland suits and dresses, the women looked like identical spokes in a wheel. The contrite mothers later agreed amongst each other to individually write brief apology notes to the teacher. But one of the letters was revealed to be long and rich in detail after it was quoted and praised in a teacher's newsletter to the class. The other apologizers immediately began sleuthing to find out who was the culprit that had veered from the covenant. A pitfall for that mother!

Especially in the early elementary school years when most of us were on unfamiliar territory, the mothers pursued uniformity with a vengeance. They wanted to be included in all the lunches, coffees, and playdates. They signed their children up for the same camps. The conformism assured them that they wouldn't stand out and risk offending someone in a society that upholds propriety. And banding together kept them in the loop of the goings-on at school. The valued particulars ranged from what might be on the next science test to where to get certain school supplies. A few hours after the school distributed a packing list for a summer retreat one year, I went to a local hobby and craft store to buy one of the items: a fishing net. But it was too late. There'd already been a run on them by mothers who had decided that was the go-to store. The day after the art teacher asked the children to bring in paint sets, I ran into a group of mothers at a stationery store.

"My daughter won't be happy unless she has the same one as everyone else," said one, squatting by a stack of them.

Even though I already had some brushes and paints at home, I grabbed the same set everyone was buying.

Obsession with the status quo exists in other school circles, too. Around the time Taro started school, a public school in Osaka, Katayama Elementary, put out an instruction booklet that answered as many conceivable questions as possible to ease the anxieties of new parents. Dozens of local schools followed suit with their own brochures. "*Katayama Navi*" (short for "navigation") is a thirty-eight-page manual, updated each year, that lists necessary supplies down to the number of pencils first graders should bring to school. It offers advice such as: "*Please refrain from buying expensive items or items not needed urgently*" or "*As much as possible, have a bowel movement before coming to school.*"

•

I was overwhelmed with trying to stay in good standing with the other mothers especially as I was starting out way behind the similarity curve. In addition to our odd family makeup, I looked different from the other, well-groomed mothers because my fashion style, bred from many years of living in the United States, was casual-practical, and I never bothered much with cosmetics. At the same time, it was crucial for me to stay in close contact with the moms since Taro often lost homework instruction papers, and I had to ask other parents about the assignments. So I attended all of the social gatherings I was invited to and tried not to express any divergent opinions. I groveled to find out about the must-buys and then sewed tiny soccer ball patches or attached charms onto the prized possessions so Taro wouldn't mix them up with all the other, identical ones. It did occur to me that my obsessive chase after the same products that other children had might send the wrong message to Taro.

"We can say, 'we have the same one!'" he told me when taking an identical soccer bag or pencil case as his friends' to school.

Was I discouraging individuality? Was I condoning the intolerance of his classmates who taunted *gaijin* because Taro appeared physically different? At that time, however, the pressure to be part of the group took precedence. I was passing on the lesson my mother hammered into me of acquiescing to the group.

August 8, 2007

"Japanese guy," said someone. They are calling me. It means a man who is Japanese. At the American camp that is how they call me, not Yataro-kun. In Japan, they often call me "American guy." (When I am really from Kazakhstan.)

One of the first orders of business for many new school mothers was finding out how old everyone was. Age was regarded as a measure of worth, with younger being better. This was not a good thing for me. As a forty-six-year-old mother of a first grader, I was among the oldest mothers in the grade. Women all over the world worship youth, but age has particular significance in Japan where Confucian values dictate a reverence for elders and emphasize differences in age. From the depth of one's bow, to the gradations of honorifics in language, to the seniority-based job promotion system, codes of behavior determined by an age-based hierarchy are observed throughout society. I remember telling a bemused American friend that I couldn't possibly oppose a certain school regulation, "because I am only the mom of a first grader." At the lower levels of the age-based pyramid there are fewer expectations of wise behavior and exceptional abilities, which is also a suitable paradigm for women in Japan's sexist society. In that sense, the younger you are, the less pressure you are under to do well, while at the same time you'll get extra praise for high performance. Add to that the global popular culture that equates beauty with youth and vibrancy, and no wonder Japanese women want to stay young. In a survey released in 2008 by the food and beverage company Kagome, 92 percent of women between the ages of twenty-five and fifty-nine said they felt it was advantageous to appear youthful.[17] About one third of those respondents said that it was because looking young made them feel "superior to friends in the same age range." On the flip side, being brazen and shameless were considered traits of a woman getting on in her years.

I certainly didn't want to add those labels to my already shaky school-mom credentials so I lay low whenever the conversation of age came up, which was often. The mothers probed each other by joking about how very old they were without actually specifying their age. That might coerce others to become competitively modest and say, "Oh, but I am even older" and inadvertently reveal their age. I managed to hold out, sort of, until one day when Taro was in the third grade. I was on a ski trip with two other families from school and was about to write down my age on a ski-class form when I sensed an eagle eye peering over my shoulder. The mother of one of Taro's classmates was trying to read the digits. I hesitated for a moment, and then nervously wrote down "44," shaving off a few years. Several days later, a mother who hadn't been anywhere near the slopes came rushing up to me at a school event.

"I found out we are the same age!" she said, smug with the pleasure of discovery.

---

17 http://www.kagome.co.jp/library/company/news/2008/img/080303001.pdf

I felt bad about lying, but I was not alone in my deceit. When *City Living*, a free newspaper for female office workers, conducted an Internet survey in 2007, nearly half of the women who responded said they lied about their age on items like train commuter passes and questionnaires.[18] So far, beyond the ski school sign-up fib, I've only had the courage to lie on my loyalty card for a neighborhood park. I'm five years younger on that one, and it's my guilty pleasure to see that "proof" of a younger age. At The School, I stayed on guard not to get tripped up in a web of lies. Japanese often refer to their birth year by its Chinese zodiac sign, so I had to remember that I was supposedly born in the year of the rabbit. And I had to resist eye rolling when yet another young mother bemoaned an approaching birthday.

April 30, 2007

"OK, here we go." I peeled the paper off the candy at the barbershop. The candy dropped straight into my mouth. My mother had said, "If you eat the candy, no dessert." But I ate it secretly, because my mother was not there. Just to be safe, I practiced saying, "I didn't eat it." The candy got in my way in my mouth so I spit it out. But she smelled it on my breath.

I thought, "Shoot."

"You shouldn't lie," my mother said over and over again. She always gives the example of the boy who cried wolf.

I always think, "Here we go again."

---

18 *Sankei Shimbun* Tokyo Edition, Nov. 7, 2007, 26 (Japanese).

Lying is great if you don't get caught, so I try to lie at least once a day. My recent lies are,

1. *I ate a tangerine before dinner.*
2. *I read a book after I turned off the lights.*
3. *I secretly ate some of the snacks for sports day in my room.*

Age wasn't the only secret I kept in my efforts to fit in. I was mum on the unusual aspects of our lives. I never told the other mothers that Taro was adopted. I was vague about my employment history of working as a journalist for the *Associated Press* and *Time Magazine*. I felt that my background was too removed from the experiences of the other women for them to understand and feared that it would prompt them to write me off as too strange to be part of their group. Occasionally a passing remark would drive that point home. On the sidelines of soccer practice one day, a mother was recalling how she had scolded her son the night before by telling him how different he was from the other well-behaved members of their family.

"I told him, 'Maybe we found you left under some bridge or something,'" she said. In her world, an abandoned child, who is what Taro was, symbolized a bad bud destined to grow wayward. Did I take the opportunity to explain the joys and wonders of adoption? Of course not. I lay low.

•

The smart mothers with time on their hands channeled their energy and unfulfilled intellectual capabilities into guiding their children through school. Not only was this a socially acceptable occupation, you could turn your nose up a little higher if you were supervising a child at a top-tier school like ours because those institutions expected more parental involvement. My sense of self was saved by the high status given to mothers in Japan as it compensated for my insecurities about not having a prestigious job title or a boyfriend. I occasionally went out on dates, but never happened upon mutual interest. So instead of a spinster with a few low-paying freelance jobs, I spun myself as a busy woman juggling motherhood and part-time work. Still, I felt I was on the modest end of the scale with my unglamorous jobs of translating and writing, and with a low-achieving son. One mother I knew was always groomed to perfection with long wavy hair, colored a warm auburn, and modeled part-time for a women's fashion magazine. In parenting, she turned every spare moment into an educational opportunity. In her car, she played scholastic CDs like one that droned on the names of the country's forty-seven regions. If we were waiting in line somewhere she would quiz her child on historical events, displaying her own impressive knowledge. When it seemed like all those exercises were exhausted, she had her son count out loud from one to a thousand. This was in first grade when Taro had not yet mastered double digits.

The mothers went about arranging play activities with similar gusto. Once or twice a year, class rep mothers would arrange what was called a "Fun Gathering." These were get-togethers on a weekend or holiday for all of the parents and children of a class. When Taro was in the fourth grade, the mothers in charge rented a community hall where they planned a day of lunch and recreation. I saw the organizers holding many meetings, hovering over Excel spreadsheets of menu items and tasks such as who would cook what, which games should be played, and so on. During a casual conversation with another mother, I carelessly let it slip that I thought all that labor-intensive cooking from scratch as opposed to ordering food was "a hassle." Within days I heard through the grapevine that my remark had gone viral and that the chief organizer was opening meetings by saying, "*Some* mothers apparently think this is all a *hassle*." Panicked by the realization that I'd compromised years of effort to fit in with one reckless remark, I went over that night to the chief's house with an olive branch in the form of a box of cookies. "Don't worry," she reassured me. "I know you well enough to know what kind of a person you are." I guess that meant that despite what I had said, she liked me and was not going to ostracize me. Still, on the day of the event I made sure to stay in the kitchen, washing dishes and slicing bananas for the hundreds of crepes that another mother was happily cooking away. And I made sure to do it all with an air of enthusiasm.

Nearly every month, and sometimes several times a month, there were events for the mothers to attend at school. Most of them required more involvement than breezing in and out. On Sports Day, every May, parents lined up at the campus entrance sometimes before sunrise in order to secure a good spot to spread a picnic sheet around the track from which to view the events. Actually, the menial task of getting a good seat was one of the few school duties relegated to the fathers since it was simple enough for a typically absentee parent to handle. Of course Taro never had a dad for these occasions. He hasn't seen his father since he was five. My ex-husband had actually adored Taro during the first three years of his life that we all lived together. He hadn't particularly wanted children.

"Do whatever you want," he said, when I told him I wanted to adopt. "I'll sign on the dotted line." But once he met Taro in the hospital in the old industrial town in northern Kazakhstan, he was transfixed. When Taro was a toddler, my ex would play with him outside for hours, so proud when others complimented Taro's coordination in chasing the soccer ball or swinging a plastic baseball bat. So proud to have a little male companion who literally looked up to him and laughed excitedly at his attention. When we divorced in 2002, I got full custody and signed a contract that stated visitation would be "as often as practically possible." My ex remained in China and started another family there. The first few years following the divorce, he would occasionally come to Tokyo on business trips and take Taro out for the day, to playgrounds and restaurants. But there were often disappointments. One day when his father was in town Taro said, "My dad is a liar."

"Why do you say that?" I asked.

"He told me he going to take me to the store today and buy me anything I wanted." But his dad never showed up for that promised shopping date.

Another time, we had flown to Hawaii to meet him. I waited for his call that never came. When I finally reached him on the phone, he told me he couldn't come and was vague on the reasons. I could hear what sounded like dishes clanging in the background and guessed that his wife was in the vicinity and for whatever reason he could not speak frankly. I told Taro his dad was busy and would not be coming. But while we were strolling in Waikiki's Kapiolani Park, Taro kept running up ahead to the giant banyan trees and their dangling hanging roots, smiling and saying, "Maybe he's just hiding behind that tree." Taro last saw his father when he was six, and they went to Yankee Stadium together. The intermittent child support payments ceased in 2008. I considered suing him but decided against it because my father was opposed, and I would have had to use some of his money for the legal fees.

"I don't think you want to get involved with that," my father said. I believe my parents feared a legal battle would sink their daughter into a world unknown to them, down into a sordid, rage-filled battle that Taro, too, could be dragged into.

October 30, 2006

Right now I am looking at a baseball mechanical pencil. A long time ago, my father took me to see a baseball game. He bought me the mechanical pencil where you push on the baseball cap to let the lead out. He also bought me a silver ball and an ordinary white ball. Actually, the mechanical pencil only has a little bit of lead in it. But I am treasuring it.

The hole in Taro's heart from an absent father was partly filled by a loving bond he developed with his two cousins. My brother's sons, two and four years older than Taro, were growing up in New York City with an American mother and a Japanese father. We often got together on holidays, and it was interesting to observe how different educational values and environments were reflected in the children. One Christmas in Tokyo, the three boys were playing with blocks, occasionally coming to heads and destroying each other's structures. Takuma, two years older and aged five, carefully articulated to Taro as he must have been taught, "Taro, how would you feel if I broke yours?"

Taro was silent for a moment, and then pummeled down the tower he had just built. "I did it before you could," Taro said.

Another time, Takuma kept asking Taro, "Do you remember what your real mom looked like?"

"Auntie Kumi is Taro's real mom now," my brother offered.

"You know what I mean. Your real mom," Takuma persisted. Taro didn't reply and seemed to be waiting for someone else to offer the correct answer. I had told Taro many times that he was adopted and how wonderful it was that he came to our family, but other than our private talks, the subject had never been discussed in front of him. My sister-in-law explained that for Takuma this was a common topic because, "every Asian child in Takuma's class is adopted."

June 20, 2008

Today I went to eat Korean barbecue with my cousins. The older brother's specialty is meat. The younger brother is in charge of movies and fun things. The older brother, Kazuma, taught me the tasty way of eating the meat. But what was really fun was fighting over the fire area with the younger brother, Takuma. You can cook the meat well where the flames are. That's what we fought over. I ate dessert with Kazuma. I want to be like both of them. In other words, fun, know a lot about movies, and specializing in meat.

•

At Sports Day, parents would spend most of the sweltering day sitting on picnic sheets on the ground, many of us holding black sun parasols while rubbernecking for a glimpse of our children. It was supposedly a pleasurable family day at school but the expected behavior of the mothers was to diligently observe the children rather than socialize. One year, after the event, I joined other mothers and teachers in my bare feet to scrub down with a deck brush the cement outdoor walkway that aligned the field. I can't remember how I got involved in the cleanup crew, but I knew it was a good chance to display my devotion to school duties. Parents also queued up early to secure good seats at the annual year-end school concert, held at a local auditorium. Each grade performed several songs, and it was frowned upon to leave after just hearing your own kid, making this a several-hour affair. At the long-distance races in December, we stood along the course in the bitter cold, cheering on every child. For the potato-roasting festival, also in the winter, the children collected the leaves and kindling. But it was the mothers who built the ground pit and then stoked the fire while the vegetables cooked, fanning it just enough so the embers remained orange beneath the gray ashes while the children went back to class. After the children consumed their feast, the moms formed a bucket brigade to douse the fire. I had a ratty coat and some old, post-eye surgery goggles set aside for the hours I would spend each year amid the smoke and ash swirling in the wind.

July 4, 2008

Every year, my mother makes brownies for Sports Day.

Brownies are an American-style chocolate cake. The brownies are just like they appear on the cover of the box. I think this year, too, my mother will make them well and hand them out to everyone.

1. *The good part of brownies is the edge. The reason is it's hard and really tastes like chocolate.*
2. *A good way to eat, together with vanilla ice cream.*

A point to be careful. It can stick to your teeth because it is gooey. Once my mother's tooth filling came out together with a piece of brownie.

I found the amount of time involved and the physical discomfort while attending some of these events a burden, but the other mothers appeared to relish the camaraderie born from the shared experiences. And, of course, you never knew when you might come across some tidbit of crucial information. Sometimes, there was a happy surprise. I'll never forget the moment of euphoria I felt when Taro's class won the fourth-grade dodgeball tournament. His class had been the underdog, having a young and inexperienced homeroom teacher, Harada Sensei, who had just started teaching the year before. Eager for a victory to boost his lowly status, Harada Sensei wound the kids up by showing them tapes of national dodgeball championship games, promising to have a pizza delivered to the classroom if they won. The children practiced for months during recess and after school. Team spirit soared. When the final whistle blew with our class ahead, the children leapt up in joy, and many mothers, including me, couldn't contain the tears in our eyes.

February 27, 2009

Today, with an explosion, we won the dodgeball tournament. And the plaque that used to be in the South Classroom is now in the North Classroom. It's a trophy for me. It's been used for a long time.

I touched the plaque. In fourth grade, I put it in my hands for the first time. I never knew it would be so moving to win.

"Wow . . ." is all I could say. If I look at it, I get a whole lot of memories. I'm looking forward to going to school.

•

We were each required to serve one term on the PTA. The duties involved organizing school and class events, running fund-raising campaigns and being a liaison between the school and the parents. It was easiest to do PTA work during the younger years when your tasks would be of a lower caliber than the leadership duties assigned to the senior mothers of children in higher grades. The competition to nab a PTA position in the early grades was settled by heated rounds of rock-paper-scissors hand games among the mothers. One determined mother went shopping at a store known for selling fortuitous red underwear and wore a pair on the big day, but she still lost. I was luckier and became a class mother when Taro was in second grade. It was ideal timing as we were given simple jobs assigned to lower grade parents but still knew enough about the school culture to avoid whatever pitfalls had tripped up that mother who had been bullied as a first-grade PTA rep. In addition to arranging a few class socials, I was in charge of purchasing juice for the school-wide PTA meetings and laying out the cartons on the desks. I also set up and put away a lot of folding chairs. Like other events, PTA gatherings were well scripted. The questions asked at PTA sponsored lectures by guest speakers, for example, were all softballs from plants in the audience. In addition to PTA work, we took on traffic patrol each semester aimed at quieting down the children en route home when they rode the public bus from The School to the local train station. Sporting armbands identifying us as on duty from the school, we boarded buses and ushered the children to the train station hoping our show of efforts would fend off the frequent complaints from the other riders about boisterous children crowding the buses. Afterwards we submitted detailed reports on our observations. I wrote entries like, "some children hovered around the pay phones so I told them to cease playing around and head home."

March 7, 2008

Things Grandmother Doesn't Know

1. She doesn't know the Docomodake.[19]
2. She doesn't know the winner of the Tokyo Marathon.
3. She doesn't know about The School.
4. She doesn't know why the sky is blue.

Today my grandmother is here because my mother is at PTA. I found out when I was walking home from piano with my grandmother.

When I asked my grandmother, "Do you know what Docomodake is?" she said, "I don't know." So that's how I found out.

At the traffic light by the apartment, my grandmother said, "That cloud is like a whale." My grandmother and I looked at the clouds and walked. When we got home, the whale wasn't there anymore. I thought, "My grandmother has pretty good eyesight." I want my grandmother to come again.

---

19 Docomodake is a mushroom character that is the mascot for the mobile phone operator DoCoMo.

At first glance, you wouldn't notice all the hard work and energy the mothers put into school affairs because of their extreme humility. One of Taro's fifth-grade classmates received a commendation for her report on a prison break by Japanese POWs in Australia during World War II. When I emailed the mother to congratulate her, she wrote back that she didn't know anything about it.

"My daughter did it all by herself," she replied. I was so impressed that a fifth grader could have done all that research, but I should have known better. The project displayed at school featured a handwritten page by the mother on her supervision of the research, and a foreword by the girl that acknowledged, "*My mother took me to the library and arranged the photos.*" An American parent might deny involvement in a child's school project to promote the child. But the same response in Japan comes from another source. The mother had been modest with me, dismissing her daughter's work as something a child had thrown together and not worthy of my attention. Japanese routinely berate themselves and praise others. Sociologists say this behavior has helped the crowded country maintain harmonious, interpersonal relations by avoiding conflict. Humility puts others at ease.

This pervasive deferential behavior has always been the most difficult cultural trait for me to grasp. Although I was raised by conservative Japanese parents and have spent half of my life in my home country, the gap between humility and reality continues to confound me. I could understand, for example, the appeal of something like the unassuming dignity displayed by former New York Yankees player Hideki Matsui; after he was named MVP of the 2010 baseball World Series, he told a Japanese TV interviewer that he asked himself, "Did I do something?" But when a mother feigns no knowledge of a report that she supervised hands-on, isn't that simple dishonesty?

I concluded that the self-flagellation among the mothers was in part a tactic to keep the competition at bay. They routinely complained that their kids were lazy, incompetent, and brought home the worst grades. I used to feel relieved that Taro wasn't the only one who resisted doing homework until I discovered that the alleged sloths were actually star students. Over and over again, I would take what other mothers said at face value and later feel duped. If it was that confusing for me, it should be impossible for non-Japanese to understand. Indeed, "reticence and humility" were among the top-ranked cultural behaviors believed to be puzzling for foreigners, according to a 2007 Internet-based survey of Japanese by the web research firm Dimsdrive.[20] As for the war-historian mother, I tried to outdo her by stooping even lower. "*The report is so advanced,*" I wrote in an email to her. "*It's an honor for us that my son may tread upon the same school hallways as your daughter.*"

•

The mothers were polite, but no pushovers. They were fiercely protective when it came to the standards of their children's education. Taro's homeroom teacher from the third through sixth grade, Harada Sensei, was a novice, straight out of graduate school. Many mothers were suspicious of his competence. When Harada Sensei was directing a class play,

20 http://www.dims.ne.jp/rankingresearch/101_150/111/002.html (Japanese).

one mother offered during a parent-teacher meeting, "You are new and might not be familiar with the plays. Please let us know when you want us to help you."

In essence, "Just hand the stage over to us." Later, a group of mothers of children in his math class confronted him about his teaching methods.

"Do you like math?" a mother who was a scientist asked. She spoke politely, using appropriate honorifics, but the connotation was sarcastic and condescending. More like, "*Do you even like math?*"

Teaching has traditionally been a revered and well-paid profession in Japan with its mission extending beyond just academics to include a shaping of the student as a whole. While the practice is declining, teachers used to visit families in their homes to check on their pupils' after-school environments. Like his classmates, Taro always sent a postcard to his homeroom teacher during summer break to report on his activities, and he always received a reply. But the dynamics of the respectful relationship between parents and teachers is changing. Some hovering and over-protective helicopter parents, dubbed "monster parents" in Japan, harangue schools with demands such as to change a report card grade, to take sides in playground fights, or to come up with a better yearbook photo. Typically, the parents phone the teachers at school to voice their complaints, but in more extreme cases, they can harass teachers at their homes or file lawsuits against them. Nearly half of Tokyo public school teachers now take out liability insurance policies designed for protection against such circumstances.[21]

---

21 http://www.newevery.com/about/#sec4 (Japanese).

The phrase "monster parent" gained instant notoriety in 2002 after the director of a day care center in Saitama Prefecture, just north of Tokyo, set herself aflame on the property's playground. She left a note that linked her suicide to the constant complaints she had received from the parents of a boy who had scraped himself in an altercation with another boy at the center. A government survey showed that cases of sick leave due to mental illnesses of public elementary and junior high school teachers tripled in ten years from 1989.[22] And dealing with parents was cited as among the top reasons of stress for principals in a separate survey.[23]

I wouldn't categorize any of the school moms I knew as monsters. But the feeling at the school was that some parents were extreme enough to fit the bill. At one school-wide PTA meeting the principal went over the teachers' daily schedules, explaining that their duties included, in addition to teaching class, their own meetings and research projects, work on various committees, and supervision of student club activities. Japanese teachers work long hours, often twelve hours a day.[24]

"I am not asking you to hold back from discussing issues with us," the principal said. "I just want you to be aware of their schedules." A mother sitting next to me leaned over and whispered, "monster countermeasure!"

I did have a few brushes with one mother. At the fourth-grade potato-roasting festival, Ryoko Tomita, a prim and

---

22 http://www.mext.go.jp/b_menu/shingi/chousa/shotou/088/shiryo/__icsFiles/afieldfile/2012/03/16/1318684_001.pdf (Japanese)

23 http://www.mext.go.jp/b_menu/shingi/chousa/shotou/088/shiryo/__icsFiles/afieldfile/2013/02/26/1330868_05.pdf, page 5 (Japanese).

24 http://www.mext.go.jp/b_menu/shingi/chousa/shotou/088/shiryo/__icsFiles/afieldfile/2013/02/26/1330868_05.pdf, page 20 (Japanese).

reserved woman with whom I had had little contact other than small talk at school events, came up to me and asked if I had a minute to discuss something.

"I know he may not mean any harm," she began, "but Yataro-kun has been doing *kancho* against Tadaki, and he doesn't like it." *Kancho*, which literally means enema, is a prank that young children, boys mostly, play against each other where they run up and poke others in the rear end with their fingers and shout "*kancho!*" It is frowned upon, but generally not taken too seriously. Nevertheless, I was dismayed that Taro was engaging in such immature behavior and, more than that, terrified of making an enemy out of another mother. I apologized profusely and told her, "My son doesn't listen to me, so I will discuss it with the teacher."

But when I told Harada Sensei, he replied, "Oh, was it Tomita-san? She's always complaining. And all the boys play *kancho*. It's not a big deal."

"But they really shouldn't be playing it in the fourth grade," I countered. "Can you please make Yataro stop?" I also told Taro myself not to play such a stupid, vulgar game, especially when someone doesn't like it. Initially he denied his involvement. Then he complained that Tadaki was a tattletale. I decided not to harp too much on the issue out of fear that Taro might take it out on Tadaki at school.

I didn't know much about Tadaki Tomita as Taro had never been particularly good friends with him. As far as I knew, Tadaki was a quiet boy who did well in all subjects at school, including sports. In the first grade, I once saw him kindly reminding Taro to have his textbook opened to the correct page before class started. Ryoko Tomita had been a PTA class representative in the first grade and seemed to handle her duties as treasurer with efficiency. She struck me as soft-spoken and reserved but capable. Thinking back, I realize there had been signs early on that she was an overprotective mother. I noticed the mother and child once on a packed bus from school to the train station. Tadaki, then a first grader, was the only boy sitting next to his mother; all the other children were standing and talking amongst themselves. Another mother had told me that when the children were in second grade, she overheard Ryoko chastising Mori Sensei during a parent-teacher conference, demanding that he take more charge of the class. Word went around at the time that she had been livid that Mori Sensei had lost some illustrated diaries that Tadaki had made over the summer.

About six months after the *kancho* complaint, I got an email one evening from Ryoko saying she was going to phone me later. I was busy packing for a trip and annoyed to have to deal with her again for what I assumed was mischief by Taro.

"Now what did you do?" I asked him. "Tadaki's mom wants to talk to me about something so you'd better tell me right now what you did so I know how to respond."

Taro told me that a group of boys were changing from their tennis clothes into their uniforms in the classroom. One of them said, "Tadaki likes Satoko."

Taro went over to Tadaki and said, teasingly, "So you like Satoko. Is that for real?" Tadaki then punched Taro in the face, and Taro shoved him back. Neither was injured. Tadaki went to Harada Sensei and complained. The teacher told all the boys to apologize to each other, adding to Tadaki that he should first try to solve his problems directly with the other boys instead of always coming to the teacher right away. I was a bit more lenient with Taro this time because I was beginning to think that Ryoko might be overreacting.

"OK, but you shouldn't have hit him back," I told Taro. "It wasn't nice to tease him, but if you hadn't hit him back you might have been the good guy. Since you hit him back, now you're just as bad as he is."

It turned out that Ryoko actually had a different event in mind. She said that Taro had teased Tadaki on the tennis court. I apologized to her about that, but could not contain myself and told her about the boys' scuffle in the classroom. Ryoko said Tadaki had not told her about that and that she was worried that he was not able to assert himself.

"At least he has the spirit to punch someone," I told her, in a sincere effort to lift her spirits.

Harada Sensei later told me that Taro's report was essentially accurate, but that he had left one thing out. When the teacher told all of the boys to apologize to each other, Taro had refused and was scolded for that. Taro's reasoning was that he had not done anything wrong because all he did was convey what someone else had said. He was just the messenger.

May 16, 2009

Today I had a fight at Inokashira Park. The other kid didn't hit me or anything. I was helping someone collect shells. A kid lent me his net because I couldn't go in the water with my shoes on. Here is how the fight went.

Him "Hey, why do you have that net?"
Me "He lent it to me."

Him "Let me have it. I was here first."
Me "Not possible. Bring your own."
Him "What grade are you in?"
Me "Fourth. What about you?"
Him "Third."
Me "If I said I was in second, I know you were going to say you have to listen to me."
Him "I never said that."

That's how it went. It didn't look like it was going to end, so I finished by saying, "Oh, that's nice" and just ignored him.
A few days later, that kid was swinging on a hammock put up between the trees. He makes me mad!

In the remaining two years of elementary school Ryoko did not complain to me directly, but she continued to approach other mothers of boys in the class to protest treatment of her son. Most of them, like me, apologized and turned around and scolded their children in order to avoid further confrontation. Ryoko also demanded that the school supervise better, claiming that her son was the victim of group bullying. Taro told me that after some run-in at the lunch table one day, one girl said, "Don't bother Tadaki because he'll tell on you, and then his mom will get really mad and come to school."

Harada Sensei, desperate to smooth out the nettlesome situation, asked some parents directly to apologize to Ryoko. One mother refused.

"Tadaki called my son 'fat' and said his clothes were uncool. Tadaki's mother doesn't know that her son is the bad one," she told me.

Another mother, whom I admired for seeing the big picture, said, "I told Sensei, 'If it helps that I apologize, I will.' But I didn't say anything to my son about it because it's all so ridiculous. The kids should sort it out themselves.'"

Yes. Ideally. But that is a tall order for children who have spent most of their lives in highly structured settings. The mothers, too, were so focused on getting their children to do well and for their own selves to get along with others that they weren't exactly role models for taking a stand.

As the mothers grappled to stay afloat, the children were increasingly swept up in competitions of their own.

May 8, 2009

"What a drag, what a drag," I was thinking as I was on my way to a class. It was sunny in the skies ahead, but rainy here. "Just maybe," I thought, and looked up at the sky. I was right. There is a rainbow in the sky. As I was looking, my mother came up on her bike and said, "Come on, hurry up."

"But the rainbow . . ."

"Oh yeah," she said and rang her bicycle bell, making me ride faster. My mother's head is empty except for wanting me to hurry and go to class so she can have her free time alone.

Now the colors of the rainbow are very clear, but it wasn't like that a long time ago. I want to confirm that. I could be the one to do that. I could even do it now.

Who is always protesting, "It's a waste of money so you should quit The School"? I have an idea. It doesn't have to be The School. There are lots of other things to quit. Juku, piano. Even if I quit those, my fate is not going to change.

V

Competition

February 2, 2009

• • •

I'M SITTING ON THE FLOOR OUTSIDE OUR BATHROOM WITH my back pressed against the door. Taro is trapped inside the closet-sized toilet with a notebook and pencil. Until he solves a science problem, I won't let him out. In some sick humor we've developed, I occasionally slide an M&M under the door for sustenance. If I sense that he isn't working, I turn off the light from the switch outside. He is afraid of the dark.

How did we get here? After hours of battle over homework. Not just today but nearly every day since he started school four years ago. On this day, I'm trying to get Taro to study for a science test. As always, it takes about an hour to convince him to sit at the dining table. Then come the numerous self-imposed interruptions: playing with his pencil, eyes wandering to other parts of the page and an escape over to the sofa, grabbing a book or toy along the way. All the while, I endure and coax while my resentment grows. Here I am trying to help him for his own good, only to be repeatedly rebuffed. The other children in his class don't seem to have such issues. At a discussion meeting among the parents arranged by the school, none of the five other mothers in my group mention any similar difficulties, while I say, "Taro is incredibly rebellious." I sent him to school unprepared a few times, hoping that peer pressure or a teacher's guidance would prompt him to work. They didn't. Taro seemed to ignore any admonishments, and I worried that if I continued to let him drift on his own he would fall too far behind to ever catch up. I later found out that many children engaged in *sakidori*, literally "grasping ahead," mastering subjects ahead of time by doing drills at home or studying them at after-school cram schools. Class periods for them were review sessions so no wonder Taro was left in the dust. To add to my torment, the fourth-grade level academic work was getting too complicated for me. I often had to research the answers on the Internet. Struggling to understand the material myself while trying to keep Taro in his chair and working, I would eventually lose rationality. So today, I have pushed him into the bathroom. I'm hoping the effective torture chamber will frighten him into taking the question seriously.

If sound travels 331 meters per second in zero degrees Celsius, and the speed increases 0.6 meters as the temperature increases by one degree, what is the distance between a person and lightning if the person hears the bolt five seconds after he sees the lightening in five degrees Celsius?

I've spent the past hour entering meters-per-hour in one column and distance in another. I draw a horizontal line between 0 and 331 and another between 1 and 331.06, 2 and 331.12 and so on.

"See how every time I add one degree, the speed goes up by 0.6 meters?" I say, over and over again.

He doesn't get it. Maybe he's not paying attention. Maybe he still can't discern the pattern. Or maybe I'm not explaining it the right way. The science test is the day after tomorrow, and if he doesn't score well, he won't get an A on his report card. So what if Taro doesn't get an A in fourth-grade science? Even in my enraged state, I know that it isn't the end of the world. But I also know that a good grade will make him happy and raise his self-esteem. Maybe that would motivate him to study? If I pause to think, I know that so far with Taro, the joy of getting high marks has never resulted in any impetus to study. But I maintain my faith that it just might kick in this time. I also know that a good grade would make me proud, not just of his achievement but also of my boosted standing among the mothers. Taro scored the second highest in his class on a science test recently, and I basked in the satisfaction I felt when the others complimented me on his achievement. Even better, the mother of the kid who came in first was a scientist, which I considered an unfair advantage.

But none of this is on my mind right now as I lean against the bathroom door, pushing hard when Taro tries to force it open from the other side. I'm panicking about the test and worrying about the other assignments. In addition to science, there's a test in reading comprehension and ancient poetry this week. Next week: identifying Japan's forty-seven prefectures and city governments, a demonstration of weighing items on a balance scale and a 1.5-kilometer race. It's approaching nine in the evening, and we still haven't had dinner.

February 15, 2008

Things don't bounce that well on it, but a light thing will bounce on this sofa. I read manga on the sofa. That is what I do when I have free time at home. There is a white blanket on the sofa. This is a place where my mind can rest.

•

The School sits at the traditional end of the spectrum in the country's debate over the best approach to education: the orthodox path of memorization checked by straightforward testing versus a more flexible approach that encourages creativity and innovation. Regurgitating facts has long been a prized skill in Japanese schools because of the country's rigorous university entrance exams. But from around the 1980s, there was growing criticism that such one-dimensional learning, dubbed "*tsumekomi*" or "cramming," was producing people who couldn't think out of the box. In response to such charges, the country cut back school hours and pared curricula under the slogan "*yutori*," or "leeway." But then, the cherished high scores of Japanese students in global comparative testing of math and science began to fall, while independent thinking didn't show much improvement. *Yutori* was blamed for the slide, and the pendulum swung back to increased classroom subjects and hours. The government began phasing out its *yutori* program in 2011, the year Taro would finish elementary school. None of this affected Taro, however, since The School had ignored the movement to begin with.

Despite the struggles to get Taro to work, I still lean toward favoring the traditional approach, particularly in the younger years. A friend in New York City proudly told me that her son attended one of the best local public schools where the children learned math by pretending to run a bakery and determining the store's sales and profits. I believed it was far more efficient to have Taro recite the multiplication tables repeatedly until he has them at his fingertips, which was The School's way. "This is a lifelong skill," Mori Sensei told us parents. "It has to become like an extension of their bodies."

But I also felt The School kept some hurdles unnecessarily high. Taro loved books but often scored poorly on reading tests, stumped by typical unnecessarily complex questions like, "Divide the passage into four scenes based on time, place, character, and the feelings of the main character, and write the number of the first line of each scene." Taro had points deducted on an English dialogue memorization test once because he didn't display the accompanying hand gestures. In fact, taking the test itself had been a challenge because the teacher required the children to come to her classroom on their own initiative during recess. It took months for Taro to achieve this. Every time he walked toward the English classroom with good intentions, the sight of the playground en route lured him away.

How did our bathroom standoff that evening end? Taro eventually gave me the correct answer, although it was questionable whether he could consistently solve similar problems. We liked to have homework cleared out of the way before dinner so even though we were both rapidly losing stamina and efficiency, we plodded and argued along through the remaining assignments. At age nine, Taro was often eating dinner at ten o'clock and climbing into bed close to midnight. I had to be vigilant when he soaked in our deep Japanese tub because he sometimes dozed off in there.

•

In addition to shoving Taro into the bathroom, I cringe with shame and regret to admit that I also chased him around the apartment and dragged him back to the table by his arms or legs.

"What's wrong with you? You're smart enough. Just lazy," I'd routinely shout. "All your friends do their homework. I wish you were like them."

"No they don't," "Shut up," "I can't do it," were his common replies.

When I felt like he was nowhere close to listening to me, I lost control and slapped him or pulled his hair. Taro would turn right around and lunge at me, pummeling me with his small hands. I left the apartment a few times to cool off, also hoping Taro would feel scared being alone, but that didn't work either. He used the free time to watch TV and began latching the door from the inside so I couldn't get back in. On top of that, I worried how I would explain myself if I ran into other school mothers in the neighborhood, riding my bike aimlessly after dark or sitting alone in a café at dinnertime. When my cousin told me she put the fear of god into her daughter once by locking her out on the balcony, I tried that, too. But Taro immediately climbed onto our second story ledge and shouted "Help!" so that I had to usher him back inside before the neighbors called the police.

A few times, I refused to cook dinner. Taro pleaded and begged for more than an hour on those occasions, and his hysterical wailing of "dinner, make dinner," haunts me to this day. Taro threw my cell phone across the room several times, chipping its corner on our parquet floor. I would sheepishly take it to the shop and say that I didn't know what happened except that, "I do have a rambunctious boy at home." Taro often called my mother during our standoffs to tell her how awful I was. She was the steadfast, unconditional rock of love to him that I should have been. My mother listened and tried to divert his attention and then got on the phone with me and told me to stop stooping down and fighting on the same level as a child.

"Count to ten. Calm down. He's just a kid," she'd say. I knew that, but I didn't want to hear it when I was fixated on getting homework done. So we would argue, too, and it nearly always ended with her saying, "Well, you adopted him. It's your problem." Sometimes I caught a glimpse of myself in our large bathroom wall mirror as we were scuffling. With disheveled hair, it was a harsh, ugly mug shot of a face.

January 28, 2009

When I got home today, my mother was like an ogre and said, "Homework!"

I only had one sheet so thought that was all, but then she made me study for a test, do other studies and then study for a test that is not for a long, long time. After a while the doorbell rang, and my grandmother came in. I am going to my grandmother's house today. My mother has a birthday party so she won't be home. I will go to school from my grandmother's house. When we moved, and the new house was not ready, I went to school from my grandmother's house. I used to live in Komagome, and that is the same route to school, so I am used to it. There are some fifth graders there, too. It has been awhile since I took the train to school.

I wasn't unique among Japanese mothers in losing my temper when trying to get a child to study. At dusk one day, as I was walking toward our unit in the apartment complex I heard the yelling of children and mothers coming from several homes. One boy, probably around Taro's age, was screaming in rough language, "I just told you. I can't understand it." I could picture the exasperated mother asking her son whether he really couldn't get such a simple problem. At a Japanese film showing in New York City, I once heard several gasps from the audience at a scene where a mother threw her son's school satchel at him. I leaned over and whispered to my American friend, "I've done that and so have many of my friends."

At what point do the angry actions constitute child abuse? I don't know, but I did worry that I could be heading there if I didn't apply more self-control. Every morning after I saw Taro out the door, I would feel guilty about my words and actions of the previous evening. And when I returned home after work or errands, as I turned the key in the lock I would vow to be patient and to embrace Taro instead of losing my temper. But after fifteen minutes or so of the usual back and forth about starting homework, we would be at war again. Surely fury would be building up inside Taro, too. There have been highly publicized incidents of youths murdering their parents in Japan where the motives of the crime were linked to parental pressures to study. In 2006, a sixteen-year-old boy set fire to his house one night, killing his stepmother and younger half-brother and half-sister.

He said he wanted to destroy his world full of pressure that included beatings from his father when he didn't perform well academically. After another such case of a child murdering a parent, I was watching a TV interview of a woman passerby who said, "I can't imagine my son doing anything like that." I remember thinking that I could not have made such a definitive statement.

•

It was time for us to enlist a third party. I started looking for a *juku*. Historically, the cram schools only offered instruction to prepare students for entrance exams. But they have since expanded to cater to a much broader scope of needs, supplementing school classes with a range of remedial to advanced programs. Types of *juku* range from those run in private homes by individuals to nationwide chains including some with entrance exams of their own. About twenty-five percent of elementary school children attend *juku*, either to augment school studies or to prepare for junior high school entrance examinations.[25] At The School, most pupils would matriculate to the attached junior high so they did not need to cram for entrance exams, but many children attended *juku* anyway to advance beyond their classroom instruction. I restricted my search to *juku* that taught in small groups as I felt Taro would get distracted if there were too many other kids around. One of the *juku* I looked at offered private tutoring but in tiny windowless rooms where I felt the walls caving in even during my short

25 http://www.mext.go.jp/b_menu/houdou/20/08/__icsFiles/
afieldfile/2009/03/23/1196664.pdf, 8 (Japanese).

visit. In another, individual instruction turned out to mean that a teacher walked amid rows of desks, giving pointers to students along the way. I settled on a *juku* in our neighborhood where several groups of one to four students sat in a cluster of desks around one teacher in a large open room.

Taro was first assigned to a group with an elderly male teacher whom the *juku* director described as "a real veteran and a very pleasant man." About a month into the classes, the teacher told me he could not handle Taro.

"What is his background? I have never had a student like this before. There is a problem beyond just his academic level," he told me, clearly distressed and angry.

I was surprised since Taro had not told me anything other than that the sessions were "fine" or "boring." But while I was trying to press the teacher for more details, the director called me aside. I think he was afraid the teacher was getting too emotional and in danger of insulting a client. From what I pieced together after speaking to the director and to Taro, Taro had appeared insolent. For starters, he would not take his notebook and pencils out unless he was told to. Then he didn't seem to be listening to the teacher's explanations. The old man eventually lost his temper and slapped Taro. Rather than buckling down out of fear, which was the expected reaction, Taro sulked. I understood painfully how the old man would be driven to hit Taro, but it was unforgiveable in my mind for a paid professional to lose control. Still, in desperate need of help, I stayed with that *juku* and had Taro assigned to different teachers. Taro tested their patience, too, but those teachers endured.

"A problem beyond just his academic level." That possibility had been lingering on my mind ever since I had asked

Mori Sensei if Taro might have a learning disability. So finally, when Taro was eight years old and in the third grade, I decided to have him assessed by a specialist. The few centers in Tokyo that studied children's developmental issues had long wait-lists. I had no friends to consult in Japan who had children with similar issues, or at least none that disclosed any such problems to me. The School didn't have counselors, which was not unusual for a private elementary school. There were so many more resources in the US, so I took Taro to New York City for an evaluation.

"Nothing you have said surprises me," the psychiatrist said after listening to my rundown of our struggles. "This sounds like a typical case of ADHD."

I was disappointed to hear that. My image of ADHD had been of an out-of-control child whom no one wants to befriend and weary parents who have given up on discipline. We had just seen a mother and child like that in the waiting area. A girl about Taro's age had charged into the room, made a beeline for the blocks he had been stacking up and knocked them over as her mother looked on with an air of resignation. A Japanese woman emerged from one of the consultation rooms hovering over her son and repeatedly saying to him, "Don't touch anything." Surely Taro was not like those wild kids. But after further tests, the doctors concluded that while he most likely did not have a learning disability, he had "ADHD predominantly inattentive."

"In cases like this, we recommend Ritalin," the psychiatrist said. Again, I recoiled. It was bad enough that Taro had been diagnosed with a behavioral disorder. The idea of taking drugs for it took the condition to a much more serious level in my mind. Taro drove me crazy by not doing his schoolwork. But was the solution to give him possibly habit-forming stimulants that affect chemicals in the brain? A Japanese psychiatrist who had translated for Taro during the testing articulated my resistance this way: "There is a cultural difference in attitude toward medication between Japan and the US. In Japan, medicating (for ADHD) is a last resort to be used as conservatively and as temporarily as possible, while in the US, medication is used if considered helpful, and for as long as necessary." Indeed, Taro's American pediatrician told me, "Think of it like wearing glasses if you are nearsighted."

But I held off. During the next six months, the Japanese psychiatrist whom we continued seeing in Tokyo coached me on the so-called behavioral methods to help an ADHD child. That is, use positive reinforcement often and pose easily attainable goals. Praise does not come easily from me, I am convinced, in large part due to my own upbringing. My parents are both very critical. I cannot recall my father ever admiring anything I did, and my mother often points out my personal failures. She attributed Taro's rebelliousness to my poor parenting and suggested I look up to my brother and sister-in-law whom she said always calmly reasoned with their children instead of scolding them incessantly. If I argued back that I didn't have the support system they had of a spouse and household staff, my mother would accuse me of not being able to take criticism, which, according to her, was one of the reasons I couldn't sustain a marriage in the first place. And who was I to talk back anyway when I was dependent on them financially? In my mother's eyes, there's always something lacking in my physical appearance, too, like untidy hair or lack of jewelry. Even my table manners had deteriorated.

"That's what happens when you live alone and don't have people to point out your faults," she would say. "You need to practice by eating in front of a mirror."

I never took up that suggestion.

Was I overwhelming Taro with the endless specifications that I felt my parents expected of me? Every other week, I would report to the Japanese psychiatrist what Taro had not achieved, and each time she would say that it sounded like he was trying hard. At one point she told me she respected me for setting high standards for myself, but that I shouldn't apply those exacting parameters to my son.

"Taro might have been happier if he had a mother who wasn't so capable," she even said. She urged me to lower my expectations for him. A lot.

"Please just think it's good enough that he's alive," she said.

•

If the psychiatrist suspected that my rigid, perfectionist nature was preventing me from accepting Taro's diagnosis of ADHD, she was right. I viewed it as an imperfection, and I wished the diagnosis were, as many ignorant people say, "just a boy being a boy." But I couldn't deny that there seemed to be something different about Taro when I compared him to his peers. He was always the one child looking away from the blackboard or not writing in his notebook during class. Unlike the others, Taro didn't recoil at threats or aim for rewards. If I offered a treat for a task, all of his focus went to getting the prize immediately with no attention paid to the path to get there. He couldn't handle delayed gratification. I felt frustrated that I could not embrace his ADHD as a part of the makeup of the person I loved more than anyone else.

February 23, 2008

There is probably a professor inside the calculator. Inside the professor's head is a calculator. Inside that calculator is a professor. This goes on forever. No one thinks of things like that. I wonder why.

Hoping for a different diagnosis, I had Taro re-tested the following year at a Tokyo research center. The results were remarkably similar; Taro's ability to focus declined more quickly over time than the average child of his age. I consulted a third psychiatrist in Boston in my quest to receive the diagnosis I wanted of Taro "just being a boy." This doctor said that based on my descriptions, the rigorous hurdles at school followed by scoldings at home were aggravating the situation. To help me understand how Taro might be feeling, the doctor said to me, "Tell me something you're not good at."

I actually spent a good minute or so searching for something I was below average at when the doctor finally said, "OK, OK. Let's just say you're not a good singer. You sing all day at school and get berated for it. Then you come home for more singing homework . . ."

Up until then, I had not thought about how Taro might be feeling about his condition and diagnosis. I felt ashamed when a Japanese friend who lived overseas emailed me after her son was diagnosed with ADHD. She wrote that the most important thing for her was that her son not be made to feel that there was anything wrong with him. She said that his school should be responsible for finding the best way to teach her son rather than the son adapting to the school. And here I was telling Taro every day that he was slow and lazy and how I wished he did his work like the other kids. I was sacrificing both of our sanities to fit into The School.

Another American friend asked me, "Are you just pushing a square peg into a round hole?"

Around the time Taro entered the fourth grade, I began to consider transferring him to a local public school. The academic pressures would be less than at The School. I wouldn't have to navigate a rigid mothers' world, either. The more diverse socio-economic backgrounds of the families along with a larger percentage of working mothers wouldn't give rise to such a circle. I visited one public school that had extra classes for children with special needs as well as one private school that offered after-school remedial courses. Both of these programs for learning support, however, targeted children with much more severe issues than Taro, like children who could not sit through a regular class. I waivered throughout the elementary school years but ultimately kept Taro at The School because I felt the merits of staying outweighed the cons of leaving. The School had relatively small class sizes ranging from twenty-eight to thirty-two students compared to the maximum of forty for the public schools. Although the student body was not as diverse as I would have liked, and perhaps because it was such a narrowly defined population, The School children shared a much friendlier bond and had more pride in their alma mater than students at a public school. Even though struggling and feuding, Taro was mastering his academic subjects to at least an acceptable and, in some cases, an advanced level. I was also swayed by The School's brand name: anyone I told about my dilemma asked me why I would give up the chance to attend such a prestigious institution that was so hard to get into.

Most of all, Taro loved The School and had a close group of friends there. I wasn't at all confident that I would be able to explain to Taro why he should switch schools without demoralizing him. I should be able to say that a new environment would be more suited to his talents, but I was afraid that I would say instead that he needed to move because he had failed.

January 10, 2009

These days I am enjoying skiing a lot. Today I am at Karuizawa Kogen in Nagano Prefecture with two good friends. We can see the sun well in the mornings. We harvest icicles and have snowball fights.

"Time to go." We have to be told about four times before we finally leave. We came last year, too. We also have fights. The three of us sleep together. We ski together. "Diary time" is separate. At night we always have pizza.

We even fight over the pizza.

•

I kept my quandaries about considering other schools as well as Taro's ADHD a secret from the other mothers. Another one to add to our list of inadequacies. I didn't think they would understand my frustrations since none of them mentioned any similar troubles, and Japanese society as a whole seemed uninformed about children's developmental disorders. A mother of one of Taro's friends from day care who had a daughter in a competitive kindergarten told me she had joined other parents from her child's class in protesting the matriculation of a hyperactive classmate into the attached elementary school.

"He just disrupts the whole class," she said. I told her I thought that the kindergarten, particularly since it happened to be a nationally funded institution, should offer extra help to the boy and not simply cast him aside. Hyperactivity is an increasingly familiar term among the general public in Japan, but when Taro was attending school ADHD was not widely known outside of medical circles. Even Harada Sensei, who had just gotten an MA in education from a Japanese university, told me he had barely heard of it.

July 10, 2008

That boy is nine years old. He's a bit scatterbrained but not stupid. The boy is excited because his cousins are going to sleep over tomorrow. When someone comes for a sleepover, he quickly becomes so happy. But that boy also has one worry. Mosquito bites. Even now, there are two bites.

OK. Let me now tell you who that boy is. He is . . . the author of this diary!!

After another six months of little progress on the homework front, our Japanese psychiatrist suggested that we try medication. There weren't a lot of choices of drugs. At the time, when Taro was eight, the only medication available in Japan to treat ADHD was Concerta, an extended-release form of methylphenidate most commonly known as Ritalin. Later, Straterra, or atomoxetine, would become available, and we would also try that. Taro didn't like Concerta's side effect of appetite loss, particularly as The School's strong lunch culture valued cleaning off your plate quickly. Harada Sensei tried to give him smaller portions but insisted he could not make exceptions to the rule of consuming your entire serving. I did notice a subtle difference when Taro was on Concerta. He seemed to be able to focus for longer periods of time. But his reluctance to get started on homework remained, and he still appeared more easily distracted in class than his peers. About a year and a half after starting Concerta, Taro began refusing to take the medication, claiming it did not help him and that he wanted to be able to eat a proper lunch. This led to more battles. Amid the morning rush to get him out the door for school, I'd pry his mouth open and crush the pill against his gritted teeth. Taro agreed to try Straterra, which did not affect his appetite. But I never saw any evidence that this drug was effective. I concluded that medication was only mildly helpful for Taro and that he would need to develop his own coping methods to deal with the tasks that were difficult for him.

I continued to feel uncomfortable about medicating Taro for ADHD and felt lost amid the differences in attitude toward the drugs between Japan and the United States. When I mentioned that Taro was taking medication to a counselor at the public school we had visited, she said, "Oh no. Drugs are for children like the one who came in yesterday and took down all of the books from the shelves in an instant." My American friends, on the other hand, argued that I was doing Taro a disservice by not helping him with available drugs. Despite all the rationale for medicating Taro, however, there remained something intuitively wrong for me with this picture: a happy, healthy child with lots of friends, who is a captivating writer and loves to read, taking stimulants to meet a school's expectations. Still, the Japanese psychiatrist convinced me to keep Taro on the drugs through elementary and junior high school because the academic and extracurricular requirements are so rigidly defined during these years, offering little possibility for him to experiment with alternative ways to fulfill obligations. She felt that falling too far behind at this time could permanently damage his self-esteem.

It was easy to see how that might happen. Japanese children are constantly rated and ranked for their achievements with plenty of chances for failures to be noted. The School children received report card grades beginning in the fourth grade that ranged from an A-plus for excellent to a C for needs more effort. Taro generally had a mix of As and Bs and a sprinkling of Cs. This would be regarded as a low report card, since everyone aimed for As, and Cs raised red flags that something was amiss. In the fourth grade, there were nine subjects: Japanese, social studies, math, science, integrated studies, music, art, physical education and English. Each subject was graded in three areas: comprehension/knowledge, skills/expression, and effort. There was just one small box for only the homeroom teacher to write a maximum of four lines of comments. So clearly the emphasis was on the marks.

And school was not the only place for evaluation. "Yataro didn't get the bronze pin!" one of his classmates ran up to tell me when I was picking him from a ski camp. The meeting point at the train station was abuzz with eight-year-olds talking about who got which badge. There are certifications in practically every field in Japan, ranging from standard subjects like English-language ability to highly niche skills such as reading train timetables. One of the most popular rankings Taro's classmates aimed for were the *kanji* or Chinese character certifications. In 2006, some 438,000 elementary school students took the popular Kanji Certification Exam, competing in reading, writing, and stroke order of Chinese characters. "What color hat are you?" was a routine introductory greeting at Taro's swim class where the skill levels were differentiated by cap color.

April 2, 2007

For one second, I stood up. I can't see because there is water in my goggles. I dumped the water and put the goggles back on and did my turn. I am taking my swim certificate test. It's my second try, so I don't think the coach will pass me now. I lost my last chance. But now I am thinking maybe the coach did not see what happened. The test is swimming freestyle to one end, doing a turn and coming back. The first time I failed, because I changed arms too quickly. I wonder about this second time. When I got out of the pool, I was so tired, like when after the coach really wears me out.

"OK. Everyone passed."

"For real?" I thought. The coach did not see me cleaning my goggles. I was so happy.

Educators and parents say the ratings motivate children to reach the next level, but the flipside, of course, is that every unsuccessful attempt is a reminder of one's shortcomings. Taro endured plenty of disappointments in abacus, swimming, and skiing, where he was notified of failures alongside other children gleefully accepting certificates. I read plenty of reports glossing over achievements while stressing inadequacies such as that Taro failed a swim test despite completing the required distance in time because his knees were bent in the backstroke. I was pretty good at biting my critical tongue on these occasions, but I saw many mothers adding fuel to the fire of their child's dismay.

"Your father will be so disappointed," I heard one mother say while staring sternly at her son who had missed a climb up the cap hierarchy at the pool.

The excitement level in the lobby of the pool building on certification days was similar to when they posted the elementary school entrance exam results. The room was filled with giddy mothers chattering away as they lined up to purchase new caps while nearby stood stone-faced, angry women with the occasional tearful child.

October 14, 2007

The ribbons from America are many colors like red, purple, pale green, yellow, silver, and cream. They are ribbons I won at the camp I went to in the summer. The red one is for second place in swimming. The yellow one is for third place in crazy dives. You try to dive in the most weird way. I made my body parallel to the water on purpose. It hurt when my stomach hit the water. I also got certificates. The certificate said I improved in baseball, basketball, football, and soccer. I think the thoughts of my counselors are in the ribbons.

In addition to ranking children, the certificates offer parents the chance for a subtle boast. It sounds more humble to say, "My son is a blue cap" rather than "My son has mastered the butterfly stroke." They also help people size each other up in a hierarchical, status-conscious culture. Rankings are widespread in the adult world as well, having long existed in traditional fields like martial arts, tea ceremony, and flower arrangement. Certifications are a big business with companies charging fees for testing, diplomas, preparatory classes, and textbooks. Just before I picked Taro up from the ski camp, I myself had taken a ski class filled with badge-obsessed students. We were at the biggest resort in the country but spent the entire session on one slope practicing a certain type of short turn because my classmates needed to perfect the maneuver to win a high-level badge. None of them were in the ski business, but like many adult test takers, they wanted to perfect their hobbies. Even the instructor wondered aloud what practical use that short turn offered. One mother at a school luncheon garnered much respect from the table when she announced she had a diploma for completing a class on gel nail polish. She had no plans to work as a manicurist and said she mastered the skill to save the costs of going to a salon. No doubt the accolades from the other mothers made her happy, too.

Not only were there few words of praise for Taro during his elementary school years; he also seemed to have a penchant for angering his teachers and suffered many tongue-lashings. This was particularly the case in his extracurricular activities where the structure was often looser than in the classroom, prompting Taro to pay even less attention. The behavior that got Taro into trouble in the first place, such as not moving from one activity to the next quickly enough, was not always that different from that of the other children. What set Taro apart and exasperated his teachers was his reaction, or lack of one, to the dressing-downs. There was no visible remorse or dismay. I once saw Taro's young tennis coach lecturing him passionately, his voice steadily growing louder. Taro was looking down, mesmerized by his own feet which he shifted rhythmically from flat to balancing on the outer sides of his soles, then back again to flat feet. Luckily the coach did not catch this. When Taro was released, he seemed ecstatic to be away from the stifling one-on-one. Far from any thoughts on whatever he was being lectured about, Taro was enjoying a post-scolding high.

This apparent lack of quashed spirit irritated teachers to no end, particularly older men who were used to commanding respect, like that *juku* teacher who had slapped him. Taro had a similarly disastrous run-in with a ski instructor who had also been described to me by the ski school as "a veteran." Once again, Taro initially did not tell me about any troubles at the weekend ski camp. I was alerted when another mother phoned me to apologize that her son had egged Taro on to play games when they were all supposed to be cleaning their rooms. The old veteran scolded all the boys, but Taro had showed no sign of regret. The instructor then shoved Taro. When I confronted Taro about the incident, he told me the teacher had also kicked him in the face. I didn't see any scrapes or bruises so the assault must not have been very forceful. I hesitated to complain to the ski school since Taro enjoyed the program and wanted to go again. And I also empathized with the coach's anger. But I knew I had to speak out against corporal punishment. And the humiliation of having a foot in the face was extreme. I called the head of the ski school. First, I asked to have all the clothes that Taro left at camp in his careless packing mailed back to me.

"And then, there's another thing," I continued. "I know that Taro caused a lot of trouble, but I was also surprised to hear that the teacher used physical force. Taro told me he was kicked in the face." The principal was surprised.

"Really?" he said, but then, to my shock, he came right back to me. "Well, Taro *was* pretty bad."

Taro appeared unmoved by all these reprimands. He never volunteered to tell me about these punishments, but when I prompted and prodded, he reported them in great, bitter detail. Taro had always appeared to me as a happy, cheerful and fun-loving kid, and he still did, but by the fourth grade, I suspected that he harbored disappointments and secrets that he quietly endured. Maybe he was compartmentalizing and ignoring the realities he did not like or that set him apart from his classmates: his adoption, an absent father, a nagging mother, difficulty focusing, a label of ADHD, medication with side effects, failed tests, and furious teachers.

February 24, 2008

That sudden wind that crashed into me from the side is the weak point of a bike. Going home was surprisingly easy. That's because it was a tailwind. A tailwind is the same direction you are going. On the way over, it was a headwind. The headwind goes in the opposite direction. A tailwind feels like you are riding on a wave, and it's fun. When a headwind comes, I stand up on my bike to survive. This must be one of the easiest things in life. I think there are going to be harder things in life in the future.

VI
Darker

January 20, 2010

• • •

"Z"

The letter in red ink looms large in the margin of Taro's *kanji* notebook. It is the assessment of Taro's penmanship by his fifth-grade Japanese language teacher, Sasaki Sensei. He is a supremely confident man in his sixties, legendary for high standards and strictness. Every few weeks, Sasaki Sensei distributes sheets with rows of handwritten *kanji*. The children cut out each row and paste them, one per page, into their notebooks. Then, using the teacher's writing as a model, they copy down the characters in their books over and over again.

The *kanji* grades go from A to B to C, and then drop down to Z; a mark that shouts from the page that it is impossible to rank any lower. To add to that insult, diagonal red lines slash through most of the characters in Taro's book. The objects of such condemnation are not slapdash letters but painstakingly written *kanji*. They are not as balanced in shape or accurate in detail as those of his peers, but the deep imprint of the

140

penciled lines and slightly exaggerated angles reveal Taro's sincere attempts at imitation. But Sasaki Sensei doesn't care about effort. What matters to him are high marks, preferably higher than your classmates. When Sasaki Sensei marked tests, he wrote alongside the score, the class average as well as one's ranking. Taro always folded over the bottom right corner of returned tests to hide where those numbers were noted. Scathing comments like "Sad!" or "Don't even bother," frequented his answer sheets. Very rarely, Sasaki Sensei threw in some encouraging words such as, "Getting better," but there were only several of those in the two years that Taro took Japanese with him. Toward the end of sixth grade, Sasaki Sensei constantly told the weaker students they would not be allowed to matriculate to the attached junior high school. The principal later told me that this was never a possibility; all students of The School had the right to go on to The Junior High unless they displayed serious behavioral problems. Nevertheless, in the results of the final exams posted at the back of the class, Sasaki Sensei wrote, "wait-listed" by the lower scores and drew a picture of a red traffic signal next to the bottom five. The students' actual names were not on that list, but each score was attached to a number that the children excitedly tried to guess belonged to whom.

Amid this atmosphere of tyranny, however, most children enjoyed Sasaki Sensei's class. In a typical lesson, he would guide the students through an analysis of a story, asking them to identify the different scenes, explain the metaphors, and describe the motives of the characters. The pace is fast, almost rhythmical.

"Everyone who agrees with Satoshi, stand up," he might say, referring to one boy's answer, then quickly following up with, "All of you standing, go to the hall." The children who concurred with Satoshi's mistaken reply are exiled to the corridor as a punishment. But like a game, they are soon called back in so the next group of losers can parade out. The children sit in pairs, and if only one of them has a hand up, Sasaki Sensei might call on that one saying, "Eriko who has abandoned Toshi." The children loved the suspense of who would be the next victims and what ruthless tongue-lashing would be bestowed on them.

The mothers liked Sasaki Sensei, too. He stirred up a competitive spirit in most children that prompted them to work hard. He also used advanced materials such as sample problems from junior high school entrance examinations.

"You don't have to go to a *juku* if you have Sasaki Sensei," I often heard them say. I was skeptical about the merits of the reading tests. The problems often asked for very specific interpretations of literature. In a typical test Taro took in the sixth grade, the children read a nuanced account of a daughter seeing off her elderly mother at the airport written by a prominent Japanese writer. The main character tears up at the departure gate. The question asked: *"Concerning the passage 'For some reason, a flood of tears came to my eyes,' select from the following, one reason that does not apply to why there was a flood of tears . . . ."*

The four choices offered all appeared plausible. And you also had to remember that the question was looking for the exception. My mother and I spent many hours agonizing over which was the correct reply to complicated questions like this that Taro brought home from school. Shouldn't children be encouraged to come up with their own interpretations? Shouldn't the focus be on nurturing a love of reading rather than training to reach fixed conclusions? Such pestering of students with tedious questions could be one reason Japanese children are turning away from books. According to OECD-administered global comparative tests, only about half of Japanese fifteen-year-olds say they like reading.[26] That was one thing that Taro did do, and I didn't want to discourage his avid reading habit by chastising him for coming up with "wrong" interpretations.

November 30, 2010

I finished reading a Narnia book today. It was like the movie (of course) and the conversations were very interesting. At camp (in America) some kids said, "Narnia!" and pushed other kids into lockers. They said they would let them out right away (actually about 1 minute 20 seconds later). The locker number was always the same, and the kids who did it got into trouble.

•

One afternoon Taro brought home a postcard-sized paper that had four imposing *kanji* written vertically down the middle. It was for an exercise to learn *yoji-jukugo* or four-character idioms. The Japanese use thousands of these word clusters which when grouped together create their own meanings. Familiarity with the expressions is regarded as a sign of being educated, and the idioms frequently appear on entrance exams. Taro had a list of sixty-four of them to memorize over winter break.

---

26 https://www.oecd.org/pisa/pisaproducts/pisainfocus/48624701.pdf

Sasaki Sensei had assigned the children to write down an idiom that they felt best described a fellow student, and this one on the small paper had been bestowed upon Taro: "*Men moku yaku jyo.*" The first two ideograms mean "honor," the latter two "vibrant," and they combine to refer to a person who enthusiastically pursues goals and earns the admiration of others. "*You are so lively when playing at recess,*" Taro's classmate had written to explain his choice. The teacher requested that on the back of the paper, the parents write an idiom that suited their child. To broaden the meager list of phrases at my fingertips, its paltriness, a sign of my lack of intellect, I went to a bookstore where I found a shelf full of titles like *Yoji-jukugo and Sayings You Can Use in Conversation and Speeches*. I settled on the one-thousand-entry *Yoji-jukugo Dictionary to Bolster Your Brain*.

In my designation for Taro, however befitting, I excluded the negative ones. So out went "horse ear east wind"—the eastern wind is a spring breeze, pleasant to humans but meaningless to horses: an apt depiction of Taro turning a deaf ear to my pearls of wisdom. I avoided the praiseful ones lest Sasaki Sensei think I was an indulging parent. So I passed on "large vessel late achievement," which describes someone who triumphs in maturity, even though I hoped Taro would be a late bloomer. Taro begged me not to bring in my personal gripes against Sasaki Sensei and what I felt were his nitpicky demands. So I threw out "*ka gyu kaku jyo,*" or "snail tentacles on top of," which expresses trivial squabbling through the image of the two tentacles fighting each other.

"Shit. Shit. Shit."

When I finally sat down to write my selection, after a typical homework battle, Taro was shouting profanities, experimenting with new words he had learned from his American

cousins. "Okay. I have the perfect four-letter word for you,"
I yelled back. My mind racing full speed, knowing that I was
behaving badly, I scribbled the F word on the card. After a few,
calming minutes, I erased the tracks of rage and wrote my real
choice for him: "*jyuku doku gan mi.*" Literally, "thorough reading, enjoy taste." It means to read deeply.

"*Reading lets you glimpse into other worlds,*" I wrote in my
explanation. "*May you continue your adventures with a boy from
the American South, a Japanese soldier fighting in Burma, and
a street performer in France, all while lying on your bed,*" I said,
referring to some of his favorite books. And then I could not
resist. In the corner of the paper I drew a small picture of a snail
with boxing gloves on each of its tentacles.

May 27, 2009

*The woman in front of me took something orange out and put it on
something white and then put it back. It was a cigarette. When we
came before, I think the seat next to hers was a no-smoking seat. If
that person smoked, our family would really be in a pathetic place.*

*If my mother took a lighter out of her pocket and lit a cigarette,
I would not go home that night. I would get my train pass and go
straight to my grandmother's house. I would call the school and say,
"She is not my real mother" and be absent. Because my real mother
does not drink beer or smoke or play pachinko.[27]*

*But when there is no wine, she drinks things like cassis soda.
Actually, she even likes cigarettes. I only found that out recently.
Oh no!*

---

27 Pinball machines that are used for gambling.

•

Initially, Taro enjoyed the banter in Sasaki Sensei's classroom. He tried hard to keep up, raising his hand and taking chances amid the minefield of public, verbal rebuke. His arm was often only half extended as if saying, "I might have the answer, but please don't call on me." Hoping to keep that momentum going and get some advice on how to handle the daily homework fights, a few months into the fifth grade, I requested a meeting with Sasaki Sensei to discuss Taro's issues. Sasaki Sensei asked Taro to join us. Sasaki Sensei and I sat facing each other, seated in the small steel-framed wooden student chairs. When Taro arrived one minute late, Sasaki Sensei yelled at him to hurry over. He abruptly grabbed Taro by the collar and bellowed, "Is it true that you are rude to your mother?" I was shocked by the rough action and volume of his voice but was not afraid as I could tell that Sasaki Sensei was putting on an act. Taro, however, appeared terrified.

"Yes. No. I mean, I don't know," he said, standing and trembling like a small bird in the hand of a giant.

"OK. You can go home," Sasaki Sensei said, and Taro darted out of the room.

Sasaki Sensei shifted sideways, leaning his left arm against the back of the chair and began lecturing how Taro was essentially a good boy who would improve over time. In a swipe at Taro's previous teachers, Sasaki Sensei lamented that Taro's penmanship had not been properly supervised until now and that valuable time had been wasted. He also boasted that just that morning he had caught a boy teasing another boy in the bathroom and slammed the culprit against the blackboard to scare him into submission. I noted uncomfortably the detail on physical punishment but let it go as unrelated to my concerns about Taro. Sasaki Sensei pontificated away as I sat stiffly, nodded, and took notes. He told me he would introduce a tutor who was equipped to handle a wide variety of children.

"But he will charge that much of a price," he said. "It's up to you."

The expensive hire would be Taro's third tutor that year. In the fifth grade, I had started using tutors once a week to relieve myself from homework superintendent duties. I had wanted to escape the perennial battles and also needed the extra time for myself as I had taken on a new job. In addition to my translation and column writing, I had started teaching English two days a week at Japan's diplomatic training institute. Our first tutor was a young man, fresh out of university, introduced to me by a journalist friend who had used him for her son. I had Taro and the tutor work at the desk in Taro's bedroom which was within earshot from anywhere in our two-bedroom apartment. Yoshimasa Hagitani tried hard to keep Taro focused in the sessions, and it worked the first few times. But after several weeks, I could hear him pleading with Taro, who kept flopping onto his bed next to the desk and asking unrelated questions. I told Yoshimasa he could be firm with Taro, hoping that threats from a male figure might prompt cooperation. Soon I heard Yoshimasa yelling in rough language, "I'm telling you, sit down!"

The loud voice of a grown man intimidated me, but to my surprise, Taro yelled right back, "No way." I couldn't rationalize paying money for a shouting match and relieved Yoshimasa.

Next, I tried a young woman referred to me by Taro's psychiatrist. Teruko Hisada was a university psychology major who told me she was well-equipped because she had worked with autistic children in the past. Her method was to never get angry and to shower Taro with positive reinforcement. Teruko asked that I drape a sheet over the bookshelves and anything else in sight that could distract him, which made the room look like a summer house shuttered for the season. She kept a chart that listed a series of rewards for various achievements. It was all good in theory. But Taro didn't take the bait. I heard lengthy periods of silence—he was probably reading on his bed—broken by her occasionally saying, "I'm just going to be waiting here for you until you are ready." I think we both sensed the fruitlessness of the sessions, and I asked Teruko to stop coming.

Our third try was the recommendation by Sasaki Sensei. Tanaka Sensei was a retired elementary school headmaster who charged more than one-hundred dollars per hour, twice the going rate. A few weeks after he started, he told me that he had been a former headmaster at The School. I don't know why he or Sasaki Sensei didn't tell me that earlier. I guess they expected me to know all the former headmasters at The School. But once again, I failed the Japanese test of sniffing out the unspoken. Tanaka Sensei appeared to be in his seventies and seemed used to being treated with deference.

"I don't know anything about you," he said the first time I phoned him, chastising me for not offering a more detailed self-introduction. Perhaps because he had a connection to

Sasaki Sensei, Taro sat obediently through his lessons with Tanaka Sensei. At the first session, Tanaka Sensei looked Taro in the eye and shook his hand.

"You're going to work hard, aren't you?" he asked. Tanaka Sensei brought a lot of his own teaching materials, handwritten in beautiful penmanship, and taught Taro some fun and possibly useful things like how to rhythmically recite pi into the dozens of decimal places. But my priority was getting Taro's homework assignments completed. Current day math techniques and Sasaki Sensei's convoluted reading comprehension tests seemed to stump Tanaka Sensei who brushed them aside as too advanced for Taro's grade level. I had a strange exchange with Tanaka Sensei one day, before my mother was going to arrive at my apartment while I went out. After I told Tanaka Sensei to expect her, he kept asking me how old she was. When he didn't seem satisfied with my vague replies of "old" or "elderly," I finally told him she was in her seventies. That evening he arrived with a box of *namayatsuhashi*, a doughy rice flour dessert from Kyoto. He had wanted to present a gift and had been worried about the quality of her teeth. My mother happens to be very active and youthful, still with a full set of her own teeth. His gentlemanly courtesy aside, since Taro wasn't getting his homework done, after a few months I wiggled out of continued sessions by requesting an extended break for an exhausted child.

Finally, I encountered Ruri Yamada through a friend who had employed her for her sons and who praised her skills and compassion. Ruri and I first met at a coffee shop. I was struck by our physical similarities: tall and thin with simple makeup and dress. When we met, we were both wearing black T-shirts and black slacks. We sat down in a booth, and I launched into my history of troubles: Taro's resistance to doing homework and his defiance of all of his past tutors. As I was speaking, Ruri listened quietly, expressionless, and I began thinking that she would say that she could not handle a child like that.

Instead, she said, "It's so uncanny. He sounds exactly like my son." Her son never did his homework, routinely forgot to bring school notices home, and Ruri had braced herself to take care of him into adulthood when he suddenly turned himself

---

around during high school. I asked her how she had maintained her patience with him until then. Didn't she lose it like I did?

"It might sound like a cliché," she said, "but I viewed him as a gift from God and just accepted him as he was."

April 9, 2009

On the way home from school I caught a cherry blossom. When I put it against my lip and blew on it, it made a really nice sound. It sounded like the cry of a waterfowl. By the time I got home, I could make the sound peeeee.

I thought, even if it's the first time I am trying it, "It's thrilling." I was as happy as if I had learned to do a new whistle.

When I blew in peee, *the sound comes back* pee, pee, pee, pee *even though it gets softer along the way.*

Now the cherry blossom is as good a playmate as the azalea (I can suck honey from azaleas).

Ruri accepted Taro, too. Instead of insisting that he sit at his desk, she would read him questions out loud as he lay on his bed if that was where he wanted to be. I was aghast to see Taro lying on his back on his bed, hands clasped behind his head and legs crossed with one sticking disrespectfully upward. Ruri stood on one side with an open drill book and posed questions. Instead of forcing him to write down notes on cards, she read test materials out loud to him and had him reply verbally. It wasn't the most efficient way to study, but Ruri reasoned that it was more effective than spending hours fighting with him.

She seemed to like Taro, too, and believed in his innate intelligence. A professional tutor with many years of experience, she was knowledgeable about the materials Taro was studying. And she never came even close to losing her cool. Ruri worked with Taro once a week through the rest of elementary school. He

---

attended cram school one night a week and the remaining five days he was stuck struggling with me. That made for five nights of fighting, and two of relative calm.

October 15, 2010

Today is the night before the School Fair, but I fought with my mother until 10 o'clock. I finally thought I could sleep, but now she says I have to write my diary.

Now I can finally sleep.

•

In Sasaki Sensei's class, not only did the children have to perform well on their homework and tests, they also had to hand in assignments to exactly the right place at the right time. The *kanji* notebooks had to be put in a specified box before classes began in the morning and picked up from there later by a fixed time. Anything left behind would be thrown in the trash. One day, Sasaki Sensei took the notebook of a boy who had been late several times handing in his work and ripped it up in front of the class, destroying months of diligent penmanship, and threw the scraps of torn paper in the garbage bin. His mother immediately made a new notebook, photocopied all of the previous sheets of model *kanji*, cut and pasted the rows into the book, and had her son redo all of the drills. A few months later, Taro lost his notebook. Since the particular notebooks used by Sasaki Sensei were not sold in normal stores, I asked his homeroom teacher for one, but he told me he had already given all the spares he had to other mothers whose children had lost their books. I eventually found one in a specialized bookstore and enlisted the help of my girlfriend Yuko to recreate the notebook. I'd known Yuko since college. With two older children, she was a trusted outsider mom. I treated Yuko

---

to lunch at an Italian restaurant, and we spent the afternoon there working with photocopies of Sasaki Sensei's *kanji* rows, using scissors and glue to create a new notebook. Yuko lifted my mood by joking that my penmanship had improved from a B-minus to an A-minus with all the careful correspondence I had written to The School over the years. I felt at peace with a growing anticipation that our ambitious remedial project was sure to be rewarded. Taro managed to rewrite about a quarter

---

of the *kanji*. But when he tried to hand in his progress thus far, Sasaki Sensei told him he would not look at anything unless it was complete. Effort amounted to nothing.

June 10, 2010

I just heard my mother cry out something so I went to see. There was a slug inside the cabbage.

This is a small incident. The slug, about three centimeters long, is sliding away. My mother took a tissue and grabbed and squeezed.

"Squish."

It is a tiny sound. One life was lost in a place that only the two of us know.

Sasaki Sensei often called on the children to judge each other's work. I assumed it was his way of involving the children in disciplining procedures or trying to get them to be more aware of the consequences of their actions. But I felt that fifth graders were too young for such methods to be effective, and that if anything, the instruction encouraged them to turn against one another. One test day, he told the class that only the students who had received certain marks on a previous assignment would be eligible to take the test. That put pressure on the children to quickly clear that hurdle to avoid getting a zero for a test not taken. Taro and another boy admitted they had not attained the passing grade yet and sat out the test. The next day, the other boy handed in a perfect assignment while Taro failed again to make the grade. Meanwhile Sasaki Sensei found out that a third boy had lied and taken the test even though he had not gotten the required marks. Sasaki Sensei told that boy to ask Taro if he thought it was okay to lie and whether Taro would forgive him. Confronted with the option of betraying a friend or angering his teacher, Taro said in a tiny voice to the boy, "Sorry," and then declared out loud, "I won't forgive you."

It's not surprising then, that on another occasion Taro would be at the receiving end of a classmate's disapproval. In late January during the fifth grade, Taro came home from school, walking in the door and calling out his usual greeting "*tadaima,*" ("I'm home,") a bit more softly than usual. He threw his heavy satchel onto his bed, sat down beside it, opened the bag and tossed out two letters, one addressed to each of us. He reached inside again and took out his white gym shirt. As usual, it was soiled with sand and dirt from the school playground, but it also had a smattering of blood running down the middle.

"A nose bleed," Taro said, "from the teacher."

Just a few days earlier, I had been at a lunch where the mothers were gossiping about how Sasaki Sensei had hit children in the past until they got a bloody nose. A flicker of dread went through me as I suspected that Taro had become a victim of physical abuse. I pieced together what had happened from Taro's account, which was full of holes, and reports from several mothers I spoke to later who had heard about the incident from their children.

"Raise your hand if the person next to you has a messy notebook," Sasaki Sensei had said to the class. At first no one moved, but after he threatened to do an inspection himself and reprimand anyone who was found not reporting a sloppy writer, a few children put up their hands, including the girl sitting next to Taro. Declaring Taro's notebook as messy indeed, Sasaki Sensei passed it around the class for the other kids to examine.

"Handle with care! That's my treasure," Taro cried out jokingly.

Sasaki Sensei ordered him out to the hallway. When Taro returned to the classroom, Sasaki Sensei shouted at him, "Stop sulking." When class ended, Sasaki Sensei told Taro to go with him into an empty classroom. He pushed Taro against the wall and yelled, "Why is your writing so bad?" He began slapping Taro's cheeks back and forth, stopping only when blood trickled out from his nose. Sasaki Sensei then took a handkerchief out of his trouser pocket and handed it Taro.

"Wash your face before going to next class," he said.

Sasaki Sensei's letter to me got right to the point.

"*He was so slack today that I spoke to him harshly,*" it started. "*I believe it really sunk in today. He needs to soon be able to take more initiative in judging and taking care of himself, or it will be too late.*"

There was no mention of the corporal punishment. The letter to Taro was written with large, bold strokes.

"*Take more charge of yourself. Build up your strengths as a young man, one by one.*"

Sasaki Sensei was trying to encourage us in his own militaristic way, but Taro seemed to be in a daze from shock. I was in a panic about how to respond.

Sitting at the foot of Taro's bed where he lay on his side absorbed in a book, I let out a big sigh. Now what? I had a bunch of rapid-fire reactions, in no particular order. I would have to write a reply, and it couldn't have any grammatical mistakes in it. I'd have to wash the handkerchief. My heart went out to my bumbling son, who despite appearing stoic now, must have trembled in fear in that empty classroom. What about the tattling girl next to him whose mother probably doesn't know that her daughter betrayed Taro but with whose family we were scheduled to go on a ski trip in a few weeks? Not that I would blame her under the circumstances. And how all the mothers would be gossiping over this one!

I collected myself and assessed my options. Should I take action against the teacher? Corporal punishment is actually a crime in Japan, but the school seemed to turn a blind eye to it; another teacher who had once hit a boy and caused him to get stitches still remained on the faculty. I didn't want to get into a confrontational relationship with the school while Taro was still a student there. I also didn't doubt that Sasaki Sensei had his own good intentions, perverted as his expression of them were. The other mothers probably wouldn't support me anyway, since they liked Sasaki Sensei and would want to maintain good ties with the school. So any protests by me were not likely to get much support. One mother later told me, "I think they were both at fault," reasoning that while the teacher was harsh, Taro hadn't acted remorseful enough either.

First, I went to work on Taro's shirt, mechanically scrubbing the bloodstain with a soap bar and brush before throwing it into the washing machine. I later wished I had photographed it for evidence should I need it one day or at least to have a reminder of the incident. I handwashed and pressed Sasaki Sensei's handkerchief. As I pushed down on the iron I felt ashamed that I was following protocol instead of taking a principled stance on behalf of my son. Next, the letter. I wasn't confident I could compose a rational reply, so I phoned my mother and asked her if she could write one for me.

"He'll probably slug you next if you don't write it yourself," she said.

"*Thank you very much for the letters today to me and my son,*" I began. "*I deeply appreciate your sincere concerns about my son and for your constant, wide-ranging instruction.*" In the next paragraph, I agreed with all of his criticisms of Taro. But I added that I strongly believed Taro needed care and kindness, too. In the following, longer section, I stood up for Taro, listing the challenges of school from his point of view. "The level of his work may be low, but he is working harder than ever before. And it takes extra effort for a boy with ADHD to focus. He comes home exhausted every day. Just sitting through class and interacting with his classmates all day is a feat for him. Taro does not say much, but he seems increasingly frustrated with aspects of his personal life: a single mother who is always rushing and scolding him, the absolute lack of contact from a father he idealizes in his fuzzy memories, and the distressing fact of being adopted. Under such circumstances," I continued, "*there are signs that Taro is developing an inferiority complex.*" I quoted one of his diary entries where he wrote that he was "hopeless" in the school long distance race. His goofing off—I was referring to instances like his saying, "that's my treasure"—were probably attempts to diffuse the tension. I then wrote, "*Taro is a kind, pure-hearted and happy child who loves books. I hope the school will not crush those strong points and that he can enjoy school life while attaining at least the minimal skills to become a responsible member of society.*" In other words, having a perfect *kanji* notebook was not my top priority.

Only near the end, did I broach the subject of the hitting. "*I believe you had your own reasons for inflicting corporal punishment today,*" I wrote. "*But I think it is unlikely that Taro will become more self-aware as a result. I hope that you will not raise a hand against him again.*" My closing line was an apology for the letter being typed as opposed to the more polite handwritten form. (I hadn't wanted to rewrite the letter every time I made a mistake, and I figured my Japanese penmanship would probably rate a Z.)

I thought it was a pretty good letter: respectfully giving Sasaki Sensei credit where it was due but making my stance clear. It was polite and calm. (Although to my horror, a few days later I noticed there was a typo.) I placed the letter in an envelope along with the crisply ironed handkerchief. I gave it to Taro to give to Sasaki Sensei, and sent an email to the homeroom teacher Harada Sensei asking him to make sure Taro submitted the letter. (I had once found a carefully drafted apology note I had written to a teacher scrunched up in the back of his desk drawer at school months after the fact.)

I never received a reply from Sasaki Sensei.

The morning after the incident, for the first time ever, Taro wasn't enthusiastic about going to school.

"I have a stomachache," he said, as he slowly spooned in his cereal.

"Do you want to take a day off, then?" I asked.

But from the way his eyes lit up and he smiled as he replied, "Really?" I concluded he was in good shape and sent him on his way. A part of me wanted to give him a break, but I was afraid we might head down a slippery slope of playing hooky if I let him skip school when he was well enough to attend.

I expected the phone to be ringing off the hook with mothers eager to hear how Taro fared. And in addition to hunger for gossip fodder, might there be some concern for us? But there was a puzzling silence.

"They don't want to get involved," my friend Yuko told me. Her take was that the moms didn't want to have anything to do with any confrontation with the school.

"But it's not like I'm starting a petition," I protested.

Just one mother had phoned me the night of the incident to ask if Taro was okay. And one other mother, Shizuko Yoda, a rare lone wolf type who did not hang out with the other parents, did something extraordinary. She took a stand. Later she told me that when she heard what had happened, she went to the school with her son who was in the same grade as Taro but had a different homeroom teacher. Her son began crying as he recounted the story of the beating to his teacher. The teacher, who was friendly with Sasaki Sensei and about the same age, appeared disturbed. But he ended the session by saying, "There's nothing I can do about it. I can't say anything to him."

Apparently, the other faculty members were afraid of Sasaki Sensei, regarding him as an intractable and outspoken teacher who wouldn't hesitate to berate anyone who disagreed with him. Shizuko had taken with her a photocopy of a newspaper series chronicling my father's life, from his childhood during World War II to his various business accomplishments. "This is the kind of family Taro comes from," she told the teacher as they stood up to leave. "You should read it."

The day after the incident, Harada Sensei, Taro's homeroom teacher, had sent me an email saying he was aware of what had taken place and had reported it to "the people above." I assumed he had told the principal. Although I had decided not to lodge any formal protest against the school, I was surprised and angry that Sasaki Sensei had not responded to my letter and that the school had not contacted me with an apology or at least an expression of concern. So, two weeks later, I emailed Harada Sensei, "I just want to clarify," I wrote. "Did you mean the principal when you wrote 'the people above'?" To my surprise, he told me that the incident had only been mentioned at the regular daily meeting among the grade's four homeroom teachers, which included Sasaki Sensei.

I went to see the principal. He appeared nervous, stating he had just heard about the case and that of course the school did not condone physical punishment. I assured him I was not planning to sue the school, but that I wanted to make sure it didn't happen again. I pointed out that on page twenty of a comic book distributed to all students about the school's history, the hallowed founders criticize corporal punishment as something that would not happen at The School.

"Thank you for remaining calm," the principal said to me over and over again.

I had no further contact with Sasaki Sensei. If I passed him on campus, I averted my eyes. Taro, however, resumed his enthusiasm, bounding off to school each morning, happily participating in Sasaki Sensei's class, too. Or at least, that is what I thought at the time. I was shocked to read an essay he wrote two years later at a summer school English-language program in the US. The students were asked to argue for or against the use of spanking for discipline. Taro wrote in his still-halting English the following against physical punishment.

The last reason is you are forcing the student to hate you. I have an experience. Because my handwriting is not neat, the teacher called me to an open classroom. He kept on shouting. I could not do anything because I tried my best and I was scared. The teacher pushed me into a corner. He slapped or punched me. I do not remember. I was on the ground. With my bloody nose. Now I hate that teacher. I don't even speak back when he says hello to me.

How could I have not noticed that Taro was so wounded and angry? I had been so caught up in my own dealings with the school that I had simply assumed he was carrying on as his usual happy-go-lucky self, blocking out those unpleasant truths.

April 5, 2010

What kind of a [first-grade] partner will I get, how should I deal with him, I don't really know. And it's important what they will say about me as the oldest grade in the school. The first graders have five more years here, and we have 365 days. It's the first time I have felt that school is so much fun. I think my partner will make school an even more fun place.

VII
Last Years

May 20, 2010

* * *

I WAS BLOWN AWAY WHEN TARO TOLD ME HE WANTED TO DO HIS sixth-grade graduation thesis on Japan's human torpedoes, the manned missiles that crashed themselves into enemy ships toward the end of World War II. That's a staggering theme for an eleven-year-old boy growing up in an officially pacifist country. Japan's constitution renounces war, and the country has armed forces only for defense. Could Taro possibly fathom a time when thousands of frenzied young men signed up for missions that meant certain death in the name of the emperor and their country?

In the "*kōgakunen*" or "higher school years," the students were urged to be aware of their mature status and take on leadership roles. They were each assigned a first-grade partner to supervise, headed school committees, and wrote a graduation essay and thesis. At PTA meetings, the school asked parents to instill a sense of responsibility in their children appropriate for upperclassmen.

I was pleased with Taro's intellectual choice for his thesis but worried that he wouldn't be able to pull it off. Nationalism is a remote concept for Japanese children. The flag and anthem remain controversial symbols of wartime militarism. The government encourages schools to raise the flag and sing the anthem, but I never saw The School mandate those acts. To this day, Taro cannot recite the lyrics of the Japanese anthem even though it happens to be the shortest in the world with only eleven measures.

"How about the history of soccer or what about sumo?" I suggested to him.

But Taro didn't budge, so I decided to watch and assist. And assist I did with all-out effort. Japan is small enough that it was manageable for us to travel to many of the places Taro researched. I began arranging mother-and-son field trips with a vengeance. It made me feel good to think we were embarking on adventures together, and I also hoped that a travel record in his report would boost his grade.

The human torpedoes were named *kaiten*, literally "turn heaven" and shorthand for "shake up the heavens and change the course of the war." The dramatic words reflected Japan's unrealistic and desperate desire to reverse the steady string of US victories in the Pacific in the early 1940s. Many Japanese today don't know about the one hundred some men who embarked on the secret one-way submarine missions, their legacy overshadowed by the far better known kamikaze pilots who flew their planes into US warships. I ordered obscure books and planned trips to museums, learning the history for the first time myself. The *kaiten* were the brainchild of two Imperial Navy officers who eyed the stockpiles of torpedoes sitting in sheds after Japan had shifted its focus of fighting from sea to air. The missiles were redesigned to have a tiny pilot's chamber, an engine, and a gyroscope so they could be steered into their targets. The torpedoes began shipping out in 1944, the year before Japan's defeat.

To get a firsthand look at a *kaiten*, we visited Tokyo's Yushukan military museum. There was a notable number of police guarding the area as the museum sits on the grounds of Yasukuni Shrine, which is controversial for deifying Japan's war dead and often the site of protests. The sleek *kaiten* missile on display, nearly fifteen yards long, was striking in its length compared to the narrow one-yard-diameter opening the soldiers would squeeze into. Painted in white on the hatch was a chrysanthemum floating on water, the family crest of a samurai loyal to the emperor. "The 1.5 tons of explosives in its bow instantly sank a ship," read the museum pamphlet. What it didn't say was that the more than one hundred *kaiten* launches resulted in only two major sinkings of enemy vessels. The torpedoes had limited maneuverability and often set out at night from their mother ships amid rough waters. US ships frequently detected the submarines carrying the *kaiten* before they could even be deployed. More than a dozen pilots died during training missions by ramming their missiles aground.

"Over here, Taro," I called out to him as we were wandering amid the displays of kamikaze planes and submarines. "It's the thing we saw on TV."

We had watched a documentary about the *kaiten* that featured one soldier's farewell message to his family. Taro Tsukamoto had made an audio recording of his will before he left home in 1943. We donned some headphones and pushed the button by the photograph of an LP record. Through the fuzzy static, we heard the steady voice of a twenty-one-year-old college student reminiscing about gathering silver grass for moon-viewing parties and having snowball fights. "*I wish I could live happily like that forever,*" he says. "*But I must not forget that I am foremost a Japanese . . . . May my country flourish forever. Goodbye everyone.*"

Taro immersed himself in books filled with letters, wills, and diaries of the soldiers. The volunteers—if the men who signed up for the missions under immense pressure can be called that—were mostly in their late teens and early twenties. Their writings describe a calm acceptance of their fate along with words of gratitude and affection for their families. Some are poetic, like the one of the eighteen-year-old who wrote, "*I am the sea. I am normally calm and blue. The turbulent swirls are the angry me.*" My mother became worried that her grandson was getting brainwashed after she heard Taro say in an admiring tone, "They did it for the emperor." She pointed out that the officers were young, not that much older than he, and how they often addressed their final messages to their mothers. "*That lunch box was really delicious. I should have asked you to make some more,*" were the last words written by one twenty-one-year-old.

•

Our major field trip was down to the tiny island of Otsu in Yamaguchi Prefecture off of Japan's southwestern coast. The island had been the main *kaiten* base where soldiers trained and from where they departed. While Taro was living and breathing his research, I was the producer of the project. I phoned the memorial museum to make sure it would be open on our planned day of visit. On the early-morning ferry ride over from the mainland to the island, I studied the dozen or so passengers and eyed a mid-fifties-ish man who looked like he could be a museum director. He was seated on the deck and going through a set of name cards. I mustered up the courage to approach him. "Excuse me, are you, by any chance, the *kaiten* museum director?" My assumption was correct, and the man stood up and began pointing to landmarks from the boat, like a rock where a pilot had become grounded and an islet used for training. Good. An efficient start. I nudged Taro to pay attention and ask questions while I took notes and photos.

It was a crisp, sunny autumn morning. Giggling junior high school students were heading to school on the serene island; an ironically peaceful setting for tragic wartime relics, like the tunnel that the soldiers rode through on a tram to the docks where they took off for their journey of no return or the old cement steps that the pilots ran up and down for training. Could Taro imagine the feeling of traveling along that long, dark underpass for the last time? In front of the museum building, stone tablets bearing the names of the dead dotted the old parade ground of the base. Taro skipped around the tiny monuments, calling out the names he recognized.

"Look, Taro Tsukamoto," he shouted, remembering the voice we had heard at the museum.

Six months after he had started his research, I asked Taro what he thought about the *kaiten*.

"I can't say," he said, causing me to momentarily worry about the outcome of his report. But then he explained, "You can't describe in words how sad it is."

I was relieved that Taro had the reaction I wanted, at least on that subject. After six years among overachieving pupils and their mothers, I had come to expect Taro to not only memorize the material for tests, but to have what I felt was the correct interpretation of historical events. I could never tell with him. On our way back to Tokyo from the *kaiten* town we visited Hiroshima, which was along the route. At the Peace Memorial Museum, we watched a documentary film of the immediate aftermath of the 1945 atomic bombing of the city that showed footage of cadaver dissections. I wondered if those scenes were too gruesome for Taro, but the first thing he asked me when the lights went on was, "When are we going to eat the pancakes?" referring to a local delicacy. I tracked down an elderly survivor of the bombing who, as an oral historian, recounted his experience to youths.

"I usually only speak to groups of school children," he told me when I phoned him. But he agreed to meet us after I told him how important I felt it was for my son and that we would travel to his home. We sat in his living room as he tearfully recounted how he regretted to this day that youthful defiance had stopped him from going to his father's side as he lay dying in the next room, mutilated by glass shards and burns from the bomb. I fought back my own tears as the man showed us his graphic paintings of those horrible days of the aftermath and looked at Taro through the corner of my eyes to see his reaction. I was mortified to see him picking his nose and occasionally dozing off. Still, it seemed something did resonate.

October 3, 2010

This is something I saw at the Peace Museum. When a five-year-old was riding his tricycle, the atomic bomb was dropped. The father thought the boy would be lonely if they put him in a grave,

so he buried the boy in the yard with the tricycle and a warrior
helmet. Forty years later, he dug it up and put his son in a grave.
He gave the tricycle and helmet to the museum. You can see them
there now. The tricycle and helmet were rusty.

Taro devoured all sixteen volumes of the hardcover comic
book series on Japanese history that I had read as a child and
which now line a bookshelf in our apartment. I wanted to nur-
ture his interest in history, so I tried to take him to the places
he studied about at school. We made weekend trips to the
ancient capitals of Nara and Kyoto, rushing through as many
temples and palaces as possible. We had down time, too, for
activities like taking in a local baseball game and swimming
in the hotel pool. Taro fed the hungry deer at Nara Park and
posed for a photo on a rock where a famous scholar supposedly sat one thousand years ago. In turn, I humored him by
crawling through a hole in a temple pillar—an uncomfortable
and embarrassing feat for an adult, but one that is supposed to
assure good luck. These are some of my fondest memories as
we "studied" far away from the confines of a rage-filled apartment. It was touching for me to see Taro beginning to sense a
link between his textbooks and real life.

October 7, 2010

The other day I went with my mother and the brother of the famous
Hiroshima catcher Tatsukawa-san to a game against the Hanshin
Tigers. It was a five-to-nothing shutout by the Carp. Now the color
of my heart was repainted from the blue of the Yakult Swallows to

*the red of the Hiroshima Carp. My mother bought me a Carp cap
at the game.*

————————————

•

Back from those lovely field trips, there were plenty of projects to be completed at school. In the sixth-grade integrated
studies class, Taro had to prepare a full-course dinner for his
family during winter break. The assignment required that he
shop for the ingredients within a thirty-dollar budget, cook, set
the table, and clean up afterward. At the minimum, he needed
to make a soup, a main course, and a side dish. The entire process
had to be documented in writing and photographs, and family
members were to write in their comments after eating the meal.
I knew we would engage in an all-out brawl if I tried to force
Taro to follow all of those steps, so I sent him off to my mother's
house on what happened to be the day before Christmas. Taro
came up with the following menu based on his favorite foods:

Miso soup with thin-sliced radish
Stewed radish and chicken wings
Potato salad
Fried chicken
Rice

*"When I looked for potatoes, I looked for ones without buds
and larger ones that would be easier to peel,"* Taro wrote in the
shopping portion of his report. *"I looked for cucumbers without marks."* Then he pasted on the receipt for the ingredients:
1,465 yen (about eighteen dollars).

Next came the recipes:

Miso soup (*"the way we sometimes make it at home"*)
Stew (*"my grandmother's secret recipe"*)
Potato salad (*"the way my mother makes it at home"*)
Fried chicken (*"as in the recipe attached"*)
Rice (*"cooked in a large bowl"*)

Beneath each entry were his descriptions of the cooking process, including setbacks (*"The smaller potatoes got over-boiled"*) and challenges (*"It was hard to peel the potatoes with a knife because they got slippery"*). The integrated studies teacher preferred a minimal use of technology, so Taro had to forego using a vegetable peeler. Fortunately, my mother did not own a rice cooker. So Taro made the rice in an earthen pot over the gas stove, which I hoped would score some extra points. I padded the report with nineteen photos of the chef at work. Six hours after he had set out for the grocery store, my parents, Taro, and I sat down to enjoy our Christmas Eve meal.

In his concluding comments, Taro wrote:

"Peeling the skins was difficult, but I think it was a good experience because it will be useful for me in the future. The deep fry was less oily and better than you get in restaurants. There are lots of ways to cook and solve problems. I put all of the leftover scraps into my grandmother's compost, and it was good that we did not waste anything."

My mother's comments were a bit grandmotherly.

"When we went shopping we had separate baskets, but he helped with his grandmother's, too."

I wrote:

"We appreciated this chance to have a memorable Christmas dinner."

With such family effort and detailed documentation, I was sure we had aced the assignment. But no. I was put in my place when I read other parents' remarks that the teacher deemed the best and published in his newsletter. We had been far below standard in articulating the magnitude of the project and in praising culinary skills. One mother wrote, *"The resulting dishes were very, very beautiful and delicious. I will never forget this day for the rest of my life."* Another mother produced the following description of her daughter making a traditional New Year holiday meal dish of mashed sweet potato and chestnuts, with visual color added by the placement of a gardenia fruit on the plate, under the supervision of her grandmother:

"It was a dish that taught us the important lessons of handing down family recipes and preparing our New Year meal from scratch. It was delicious, with a gardenia taken from our garden . . . Every day, I want to pass along to my daughter the importance of cherishing food, of clearing dishes without wasting any ingredients, of never leaving a single grain of rice, of eating hot food while it is hot and receiving food with appreciation!"

Actually, Taro *had* used a family recipe, and he *had* avoided waste by composting the leftovers even though we didn't pick anything from a garden. So, it was my failure, particularly as a writer, not to have been able to compose a report of similarly weighty flair.

Taro cooked his meal wearing an apron he had sewn himself in another home economics project. My seamstress skills don't go beyond basic mending so I couldn't help him much, but I accompanied him to the fabric shop to select his material. After thirty minutes of wandering around and fingering bolts, Taro chose a bright red fabric covered with Kung Fu Pandas, and a yellow print, also with tiny pandas, for the apron pockets. I told him to pick a solid color to go with a pattern instead of mixing two clashing designs. We argued as we stood in line to pay. When I asked the cashier for her opinion, she said, "I think you should let your son decide."

February 16, 2011

Today was the day that four of us kids had to cook a whole meal. We made dumplings, scallion eggs, and floured potatoes.

For the dumplings, all you do is slice up the dumpling pancake and slice it into strips and wrap them around ground meat mixed with onion. You steam them like that. We made some really delicious dumplings. Five stars.

The floured potatoes were also five stars. The egg was four stars. Everything tasted good.

Also, if you put the dumpling skin and floured potatoes into hot water, they taste good like wonton. The chili oil was spicy. We ate the core of a cabbage.

Snow fell down from the roof.

The last dumpling especially stimulated my tongue.

Despite the demanding assignments that always called for some parental involvement, I felt the home economics curricula was wonderful in teaching children daily life skills and encouraging an appreciation of domestic chores. But like so many instructors at The School, the teacher was exacting. When the children were baking bread during a class observed by parents, one boy in Taro's group put too much water in the mixture. Instead of using that opportunity as a lesson on how to rescue watery batter, the teacher scolded and grumbled for the rest of the lesson.

Similarly severe was the approach to musical instruments. Every year, following months of practice, each grade performed several songs in a town auditorium before an audience of parents. Selected children were allowed to play a variety of other instruments such as drums, keyboards and violins, alongside the main chorus of recorders. In order to qualify to play an instrument outside of the chorus, you had to first pass a recorder test. In the early grades, the children played the relatively simple soprano recorder, but from the fifth grade they switched to the more versatile but complex alto recorder. That instrument has twenty-eight different fingering patterns covering two octaves including sharps and flats. Taro's piano teacher and I wrote down in tiny lettering the designated numbers for the fingers next to the notes on Taro's score sheets. But he didn't have the perseverance to memorize the scales. Taro might have had a knack for another instrument, like the tambourine for example, but because he never mastered the recorder, he stayed in the chorus all six years. The music teacher was troubled by Taro's apparent lack of motivation, not to mention that he didn't want any renegade recorders playing out of tune at the concert. One afternoon he called both of us in for a conference. Nakada Sensei, in his mid-sixties, spoke to us for more than an hour. He told us how he had taken up the traditional Japanese *koto* instrument later in life and the joys of learning something new, about how fortunate Taro was compared to the mentally disabled children he performed for at charity events, and about the various complications in his private family life such as the deaths of his siblings at young ages. Nakada Sensei spoke in earnest, and his tales were moving, at least to an adult like me. I suppose he was trying to find an emotional connection with Taro. But it wasn't working. Taro sat silently with eyes cast down on the desk before him where he was gathering bits of eraser dust, slowly rolling them together to make a ball and then quietly flicking them across the table.

•

Shortly after Taro started the sixth grade, in the spring of 2010, The School announced that for the first time, it was offering a ten-day home stay program to Australia. Up to twenty children could attend, and they would spend most of the time with families near Brisbane and attend a local school. If there were more applicants than available slots, a lottery would be held. But there was no need for that. Of the 122 children in the sixth grade, only 15 signed up. The trip coincided with the summer retreats of many of the grade's sports teams, and some parents said their children preferred to attend those. Taro, too, was torn between going to tennis camp and Brisbane, but I encouraged him to take up the chance to see another country. For us, the novelty was a great attraction, but for other parents a fear of the unknown was another reason to hold back. This was a school-sponsored event, and six teachers, including the principal, would be accompanying the pupils. Yet, some mothers told me they worried about safety. Even those who signed up had a long list of concerns.

"Since I am the parent of a daughter, rape is my major worry," wrote one mother in a pre-trip survey.

One of the girls said she worried about the possibility of the toilet water swirling in a direction opposite from that in Japan. Another mother told me she was so worried that her daughter might not change her underwear every day during the trip that she was considering packing disposable sets. Many parents and children said it would be hard to go without Japanese food for the duration. The broad range of concerns illustrated to me how rooted everyone was in their orderly and predictable lives and how they harbored wild trepidation about the world beyond Japan.

Taro thrived over there. On his first night with his host family he described in his diary how his younger host brother had passed gas. But instead of getting scolded, everyone laughed. "*In other words, there is no prejudice. Therefore you can do anything, even behave out of line,*" he wrote. One of the accompanying teachers retorted with stern written comments next to the entry: "*Isn't there a difference in meaning between being without prejudice and acting out of line?*" Taro also observed, "*In three minutes, I can become friends with anyone. That's why I'm having fun.*" Indeed, I saw photos of him joyously throwing water balloons at a barbecue with local children on the day after he got there. Afterward in Tokyo, he happily told me about eating his host mother's pasta, trying on his host father's feathered military hat, and playing new games with the kids at the local school and how sad his host sister was when he was leaving. Several mothers expressed disappointment with the program. They complained about the lack of opportunities to shower and the simple meals their children were served. I could imagine that the Japanese customs of scrubbing and bathing daily and eating several-course meals each night might not be the norm in Australia. I was relieved, though, that Taro was not such a creature of habit.

August 27, 2010

Today I felt once again what an amazing place school can be. A person leaving after staying over at a house for just one week can make a kid from that house cry.

   Memories
- *She was happy when she got a piggy bank shaped like a book for her birthday.*
- *The dog scratched and licked me.*
- *The cat's fur was soft.*
- *Samuel farted and laughed.*
- *The cat was on my luggage.*
- *I got a Big Mac and a double cheeseburger and an M-size Coke at McDonalds.*
- *I played on the trampoline.*
- *I saw a crocodile and a kangaroo from a Jeep.*
- *I ate Vegemite every morning.*
- *At night we played Wii and Xbox.*
- *The cat bit me when I was stroking it.*
- *I played Wii Mario.*
- *We played with sparklers.*
- *A friend called Digby came over for a sleepover.*
- *We didn't play cards.*

- *I always finished eating first.*
- *My host mother made well-balanced meals with meat and vegetables.*
- *There was nothing boring.*
- *They always were joking and fun, and there wasn't anything like "don't play games now!"*

•

The biggest event of the primary school years was the *en-ei* or "long-distance swim." Every summer the sixth graders went to a beach in Chiba Prefecture, just east of Tokyo, and swam one or two kilometers (0.62 to 1.24 miles), depending on their ability, in the Pacific Ocean. The swim is a hallowed school tradition, so strong that it continues despite a tragic incident where a junior high school boy died during the event one year. The upper school canceled its distance swim program after the incident, but the elementary school decided to maintain it. The event is one reason The School's children are so serious about swimming lessons in the early years. No one wants to be the student who prevents the school from making the coveted announcement every year afterwards of, "*zen-in kan-ei,*" or "Everyone completed the swim."

"What are you going to say if I don't make it?" Taro asked me just before he was leaving for the ocean retreat.

"I'll say, 'Can't you even do that? What a waste of tuition!'" We both laughed, and I continued, "What did you want me to say? 'Nice try'? It's the effort that counts'?"

By now, in our sixth and last year of elementary school, such words of encouragement were relegated to sarcasm between us. We both knew that it wouldn't matter how hard Taro tried. What counted was whether he went the distance. To the relief of the parents, children, and teachers, all 122 of the sixth graders, except for one who was sick and one who had hurt his foot, managed to complete the required one or two kilometers that summer. The ocean was calm under a scorching sun. Teachers and alumni volunteers monitored the children from boats and surfboards or swam alongside them. Halfway through, they tossed an old-fashioned candy called "ice sugar" into the mouths of the exhausted students. Those who finished their swim cheered on the remaining students until the final child, overwhelmed and in tears, staggered ashore.

July 21, 2010

I just started swimming. It's easy. But 32 minutes later, it's getting harder. It's very hard. The sugar candy is taking a really long time, too. It finally came in the last half of the long swim. It didn't taste very much. There's salt water in it, and I don't taste the sweetness. I'm getting a little tired.

There are also jellyfish. I touched 6 and saw 4. It was like, "Oh, jellyfish."

The feeling when I got out was amazing. I can't explain it. I can't wait to tell my mom.

The joy of accomplishment and camaraderie from that day was a lovely peak of the primary school years. But we couldn't go out with unrestrained optimism. In a conversation among the mothers when we met our children after the retreat, one woman apparently felt obliged to say, "But my daughter only swam one kilometer."

For a child who normally swims in a pool, one kilometer in the ocean is an impressive feat. But it's not good enough if some other child manages two kilometers. And for those like Taro who pulled off two, there were always reminders of further challenges. Displayed on our wall is Taro's swim instructor's report from that day. The first two sentences offer congratulations on the achievement. Then it continues, "I will write the overall weak points," and urges him to be more aware of his kick in breaststroke and extend forward more in the sidestroke.

March 10, 2011

Yesterday my mother invited a lot of people over and had a fun time. When I came home from school, there were still people there. When I hurried into the living room, on the table were cakes, kumquats, black bean and syrup ice cream, and other food. I took just a few of the kumquats and ate them. They had a lot of seeds, but I was able to spit them out. I didn't know how my mother was going to wash so many dishes, but the next morning, everything was cleaned up. But inside the refrigerator was paradise! There were lots of kumquats and tangerines crammed inside. Even if an earthquake comes we will be OK with lots of emergency food.

VIII
The End

March 11, 2011

• • •

Two weeks before graduation and amid a rush of
farewell rituals, Taro's elementary school days came to an
abrupt halt. He was standing on the tennis courts on a cool
and sunny afternoon when suddenly the ground shifted below,
nearly toppling him over. A major earthquake had struck.
The teachers gathered the children together and led them to
classrooms where they would wait for parents to collect them.
Most of them were giddy from the excitement of feeling the
massive, unpredictable force of nature. A few were scared and
crying.

When the earth nudged Taro, I was riding a train home
after a morning of shopping and errands. The conductor
announced he would be braking hard, and we screeched to a
halt. There was an eerie squeaking sound like the creaking of
a wood floor. I turned to the woman next to me, and we both
said nearly simultaneously, "Did someone jump?" Had some
poor suicidal soul dived in front of our train? In a split second,

our carriage was swaying back and forth like a magic carpet ride at an amusement park, and we knew it was an earthquake. We have so many of them in Japan that we recognize the lurch that triggers a quick panic in us that it might be a big one. And this one was. Outside utility poles were shaking, and construction workers stared anxiously up at them. "It's like we're being rocked in a cradle," the woman said as we careened back and forth at increasingly wider angles. All of us in the half-full car sat in silence, bracing for the whole compartment to flip over. People began dialing their cell phones, but no one was getting through. After a few minutes, the swaying stopped, and the train crawled into the next station. We continued to sit, somewhat in a daze, wondering what to do next. Then the conductor announced the train was stopped indefinitely. I estimated it would take about an hour and a half to get home if I walked quickly. I got off the train and went to the station's restroom where there was already a line of women, all of us getting ready for a journey out into the unknown that was the Great East Japan Earthquake, which resulted in more than fifteen thousand deaths.

Outside, people were milling about, afraid of staying inside where ceilings could cave in. Nearly everyone clutched their cell phone even though the lines were jammed. I walked briskly because I wanted to meet up with Taro as soon as possible. I wasn't particularly worried because I knew he was at The School's large open campus with buildings that adhered to strict construction codes. Still, when I looked down at my black suede boots and saw his dirty sneaker prints on them—he must have stepped on my shoes on his way out the door in the morning—I decided not to brush away the dirt. Those imprints could turn out to be a memento, I thought morbidly. A few minutes into my journey, I got that queasy feeling again. I stopped and looked up at a lamppost. Yes. Swaying. Such large aftershocks would continue for months from this day, each time frightening us into thinking the tremor could be another big one. In front of me stood an elderly Caucasian man with furrowed brow and a sickly, pale complexion. He appeared gripped with fear. The Japanese woman next to him looked calmer as she leaned down to adjust the blanket on the baby in the stroller between them. Grandparents babysitting? I resumed walking and saw a man standing on a roof trying to fix an antenna. Not wanting to see him thrown off with the next jolt, I hurried on. I knew things were really bad when I caught a glimpse of a TV screen through a store window. The entire northeastern shoreline on the map of Japan seemed to be surrounded by the flashing red line that indicates a tsunami warning. My thoughts meandered along with my fast pace. Would the nuclear power plants in the area hold up? There wouldn't be any looting, I was sure. Not in Japan.

Back in my apartment building residents were standing around in the lobby, searching for communal comfort if nothing else. Damage at home was minimal. Our goldfish was safe in its tank although water had sloshed out. CDs and photo frames were strewn on the floor. I saw on my laptop screen that an email from the *International Herald Tribune* had come through asking if I could write a column. I grabbed my bicycle and headed to school. The workday was ending, and hordes of stranded commuters surrounded the local train station. About a hundred people were lined up for cabs. As I pedaled my way in the dark, I thought about how Taro and I would bond on the way home over our first big earthquake. But when the teacher brought Taro out, he was fuming.

"Why did you come? I really wanted to stay the night at school," he said. The children had been lounging around in brand new blankets, watching DVDs and eating emergency ration cookies. Those whose parents lived too far away to walk and who were unable to drive amid the gridlocked cars were sleeping overnight in the classrooms. Taro grumbled all the way home as I balanced his heavy satchel in the basket on my bicycle. I was annoyed that my bonding fantasy was short-lived and embarrassed that another mother and son walking nearby could hear his ceaseless griping and my inability to get him to shut up. But I was too dazed to scold Taro. Back in the apartment, we spent the rest of the evening watching TV news footage of the center of destruction in northeastern Japan. We saw waves engulfing towns and sending houses and cars adrift and orange fires in the black night. Aftershocks rattled our apartment.

"I guess it's best to be home," Taro said, grudgingly.

March 13, 2011

Yesterday there was an earthquake. It was shaking and shaking and a little bit scary. But we got blankets and food rations, and it actually became fun. But I don't like the blackouts.
Miyagi had a terrible time.

I am only alive because I don't live in Miyagi. On TV, everything other than channel 2 and channel 11 is the news.

Over the next few days, the school informed us to wait for notice about when classes would resume. I assumed it would be in a few days. Tokyo seemed largely undamaged after all and the quake, as big as it was, had not been completely unexpected. From back when I was in elementary school, we had been warned that a large quake could strike Tokyo at any time with the chances increasing the longer we went without one. Just the day before, The School had held an earthquake drill with the children gathering in evacuation spots on campus. Two days before the quake, I had chastised a mother who was saying she was afraid to send her daughter overseas to study because several Japanese students had been killed recently in an earthquake in New Zealand.

"I think the chance of a big quake in Japan is much higher," I had told her.

She and a few other moms had been over for lunch. That evening Taro marveled at the sight of our post-party, fully stocked refrigerator. And in an eerie coincidence, he had noted in his diary that we had enough provisions to survive even an earthquake. But despite the possibility of a temblor always hovering in the corner of our minds, we found ourselves, like most people, unprepared. Destruction along the coast where the tsunami struck turned out to be far worse than first thought. The number of casualties would not be several thousand as initially reported, but rather ten times that figure. Nuclear reactors would explode, teaching us how misled we had been by government and industry assurances of their safety. Panic spread. Store shelves emptied even in the relatively unscathed Tokyo after a run on daily goods like toilet paper, bottled water, instant foods, and batteries. The public schools reopened after a few days, but The School decided to close for the rest of the semester. With the majority of children commuting by train and bus, The School explained, it could not ensure their safety en route amid the constant aftershocks.

So that was it. A sudden and surreal ending to our six years of primary school. The tight-knit group of children, together since the first grade, would now disperse. The highest achievers—about ten percent of the grade—would leave to go on to even more competitive junior high schools. The remaining, including Taro, would matriculate to The School's affiliated junior high for grades seven through nine, joined by incoming new students whose numbers would double the current grade size. The intense socializing of the mothers would wind down as there would be far fewer parents' events at the junior high level to bring them together. And with their children growing older and more independent, many mothers would return to work outside the home, too.

Normally this enormous transition would be marked by a formal graduation ceremony followed by several lavish parties. Taro's grade had been rehearsing for the event, in which the children would march up onto a stage and bow to receive their diplomas and be feted with a performance of "Pomp and Circumstance" by the fifth graders. But all of those ceremonies were cancelled.

We mothers had been planning for our participation in graduation, too. A few of us decided to dress up together in kimonos that day; a popular practice since the dress is appropriately formal for the monumental occasion and also offers a rare chance to enjoy wearing the traditional garb. Getting into a kimono is a much bigger deal than pulling a fancy dress out of the closet. The robe is arguably the most complex national costume in the world. First of all, there are so many different types of designs and patterns, materials and styles, with strict rules about which type befits which occasion. For a primary school graduation, understated is best so as not to overshadow the main stars. A few weeks before the big day, I went to my mother's house to select a kimono from our family heirloom collection stored properly in a paulownia wood chest. (I don't bother keeping any in my apartment since silk kimono maintenance is so tedious.) The persimmon-colored robe I chose turned out to be the same one my mother wore to my brother's elementary school graduation forty years earlier. I made an appointment at a salon to coif my long hair up on the big day as well as for help in getting dressed. Like most Japanese women, I am incapable of putting on a kimono properly by myself. A kimono is worn over several pieces of undergarments and with numerous belts, strings, and pads that keep the sash on the correct position of the garment which in turn must fall perfectly straight and show designated creases. I took a one-day crash course to familiarize myself with the mechanics of the dress and to get some tips like how to walk gracefully in the constricting attire and how to lift the dress up when using the restroom (peel up one layer at a time).

"You want to look like a tea canister, not a Coke bottle," my instructor told me, making sure I knew the dress must conceal my bodyline.

I also went to the local Yamaha music school and took a singing lesson after I heard that one of the graduation parties would involve karaoke. Most Japanese have a repertoire of songs they can whip out on such occasions, but having spent so much time abroad and isolated from Japanese pop music, I had yet to arm myself with any presentable tunes. The teacher coached me on several female songs, but we concluded there was a risk that someone else might perform these before me and with more skill. So instead, we worked on a loud rendition of "Desperado" in my scratchy, low voice. No other mom was going to sing that one.

After the earthquake, my mother told me to forget about dressing up in a kimono as it would be *fukinshin* or "indiscreet and inappropriate" to show any hint of joy during such a tragic time. It was disappointing after all of this preparation, but she was right. I canceled my salon appointment and donated the one-hundred dollars I would have spent there to relief funds. Many of the school mothers, however, would not go out so quietly. They couldn't bear the idea of not formally observing the milestone.

"I've been wanting to hear your opinion," one mother said, when I ran into her at a café near my house about a week after the quake. At first I didn't know what she was talking about. After a few minutes I figured out that she had assumed I would be upset like the others about the cancellation of graduation and wanted to band together in some sort of protest. Once again, I felt the gap between myself and the other mothers. Of course, I wanted to experience this once-in-a-lifetime ritual. But these were really extraordinary circumstances; The School didn't want to worry about families traveling across town during so many aftershocks, and like my mother, surely felt celebrating a graduation would seem callous after the tsunami had swept away entire schools and their children up north. Still, after a group of mothers implored the teachers to reconsider, The School gave in and agreed to hold a small commencement gathering.

"I am concerned about whether we are living up to your wishes with this sort of ceremony," the vice principal said in his remarks to the parents at the makeshift graduation. Normally the children would be receiving their diplomas in the auditorium before the entire school. On this gray, rainy afternoon, just the outgoing sixth graders, their parents, and the teachers were crammed into the foyer between the stairs and the science room. Still, we all felt the weight of the occasion, the marking of the end of an era for both parent and child. Many of us, including me, were teary.

"But it is with joy and confidence that I send you all who have grown up so impressively on to junior high," the vice principal told the children, and then added, "To the parents, I am full of gratitude for your understanding and support over the long six years."

The long six years.

The teacher then called out each student's name, and one by one they walked over to the podium to accept their diplomas. Taro smiled slightly as he bowed and took his certificate. It was the same shy smile he had when he peered into the mirror and saw his reflection on his first day of school, but with a bit of restraint and missing the eager twinkle he had in his eyes back then.

•

Just before graduation, the school nurse handed back to the parents the health notebooks that contained their child's growth charts as well as observations of the student that parents had been asked to submit each year. In a lovely gesture, the nurse tied a pale-blue ribbon on each student's book, the length of which matched their increase in height between the first and sixth grades. Taro had grown twenty-five centimeters (nearly ten inches). I had entered one lengthy paragraph per grade, my penmanship improving from tiny, tight letters in the first grade to bolder, more graceful ones in the latter years. (No doubt due to writing dozens of notes to teachers and hundreds of name labels over the six years.) In the early years, I noted Taro's adjustment to school and how he was enjoying this new world. By the third grade, I was writing, "*The other children progress much faster, and we feel like we are always desperately chasing after them, one step behind.*" After Taro finished fifth grade I observed, "*He was exposed to the harsh realities of life.*" It is a humbling record of my own feelings of despair. I will forever harbor guilt about how I dealt with them: the yelling, the destruction of Taro's treasured items, locking him up in the bathroom and other crude, misguided attempts to force him into making the grade. Were these "long six years" at The School a spiral downward into negative self-esteem for Taro? Perhaps.

October 20, 2010

I was in Karuizawa until the day before yesterday. I was breathing the good air. It was fun. I felt good. Then I was eating a meal, and suddenly I was attacked and overwhelmed by a worry that I would not be able to go to junior high. Just me. Such feelings don't go away for about an hour. I feel completely hopeless. I feel angry. I feel like if things go on like this, I will fail everything. That's how I felt.

I want to forget this. But I decided I should etch this in my mind and work hard.

My health booklet observations, however, end with a hopeful tone. *"Still, he put aside unpleasant thoughts, refreshed himself, and went happily to school,"* I had noted. Such was Taro's resilience, and that trait allowed him to absorb the merits of The School, of which there were many. I believe that The School bestowed upon Taro an enormous amount of knowledge and provided a valuable social setting. He graduated with a strong foundation in the basic subjects of reading, writing, and math. Taro discovered an interest in history. Science class piqued his curiosity. He grew vegetables on the campus fields and made woodcarvings in the extensive art studio. He climbed mountains and scoured the seashore at the annual retreats. He made dozens of friends, a few of whom he will likely retain for the rest of his life. Together they will remember the passionate dodgeball games, jostling on the commuter trains, and the taste of candy dropped into their mouths during the harsh ocean swim.

The School was also a highly democratic institution and forestalled my concerns about instilling an elitist attitude in Taro. Certainly, the children came from the higher economic echelons of society, but in terms of achievements at school, everyone used the same materials and was given the same expectations. It was discouraging that praise wasn't given for best efforts, but it was not like the others were given special breaks to get ahead either. I was always lamenting, "If only Taro would do the work." That meant I believed that *if* Taro did the work, he had the same chance as anyone else of being a top student. I cannot think of another primary school that would have beaten so much into us, the good and the bad. Most of all, Taro loved the school and his classmates. Except for after the one darkest day, he left home enthusiastically each morning. So, I went ahead and purchased the uniform of a high-collared jacket and trousers for The School's junior high division.

How did Taro assess his primary school years? Shortly after he started at The Junior High, his teacher assigned the students to look back and describe what they were like one year earlier. Here is what Taro wrote:

I was having fun as a sixth grader but got in trouble with teachers a lot and rebelled against that daily. My grades were low. I looked forward to recess. I enjoy myself most when I am with friends. At that time, things were easy. I didn't have to worry about my future. School lunch was good, and I had a lot of seconds. I spent the whole year in shorts and short-sleeves.

Soon after junior high started, I watched Taro one morning get on his bike to go to school, a privilege that starts in the seventh grade. As he started to pedal in his stiff new uniform with long trousers, he was unable to contain a smile of satisfaction. For a moment, I saw that twinkle back in his eyes, and I was thrilled. I remembered the five-year-old boy clutching me from behind and cheering me on as I biked up the hill to cram school. Now it was my turn to call out as he rode away. Go Taro. Go.

November 9, 2010

I am thinking about what is outside the outside of the earth. Is it infinity or are there boundaries? If there are, how large are they? I wonder if we could see them. I am thinking these things as I look at my marbles. Marbles are clumps of glass.

I am really into my marbles.

IX
Transition

February 4, 2012

...

"WHAT WAS THE RELIGION OF THE EGYPTIANS LIKE?" the teacher asks the history class. Along with a few others, Taro raises his hand. When called upon, he lifts both arms straight into the air and bows his upper body forward. He repeats this gesture several times. "Yes! Mysticism, as Yataro so eloquently said," the teacher says. Taro flashes his shy smile, so pleased with the praise. In Japan, he would have been asked to verbalize the correct answer, or perhaps, sent out to the hall and chastised for a silly act.

But we are no longer there. A few months earlier, Taro enrolled in the sixth grade at a boarding school in Massachusetts. After seeing Taro struggle in the first few months at The Junior High, I threw in the towel. I took a leap of faith and moved us to the United States. Socially, the transition from elementary to middle school had been easy. The Junior High was located on the same, familiar campus grounds. Taro and I already knew half of the students and the mothers, as they had moved up from the elementary school. Taro quickly became popular. He entertained his classmates with his impish sense of humor. He was generous: always ready to lend a notebook or piece of gym clothing to a forgetful student. He loved sports and rallied up the school spirit with loud cheers at games. He was good-looking: tall and thin with almond-shaped eyes, rose-colored lips, and a smooth, fair complexion. His classmates loved him, and he embraced the entire school back.

Academics were another story. At The Junior High, seventh graders had nine academic subjects plus music, art, calligraphy, home economics, and health—way too much for Taro to keep track of. The academic subjects included Japanese language that was divided into two courses of grammar and reading comprehension, math split into algebra and geometry, and the sciences separated into earth science and biology. Each course had its own textbook, notebook, homework, and tests. Students were given lockers where they could keep the books they weren't using on a given day. At first, I tried to check Taro's notebooks to see if he was handing in his work. I saw comments from his teachers like, "I am waiting," presumably about a late assignment. Taro only brought a handful of textbooks home and always brushed aside my concerns about his light load, saying he had finished all of his assignments.

A few weeks into the first semester, there was a parents' meeting with the homeroom teacher. Taro's teacher was a warm and supportive young woman who taught calligraphy. After the all-class meeting, I went up to her and told her that Taro rarely brought his books home.

"What?" she said in disbelief.

She brought out a master key, and we ventured over to his locker in the hallway outside the classroom. When she opened it, several textbooks tumbled out onto the floor. The locker had been packed with gym clothes, shoes, books, and notebooks, many of which Taro should have been bringing home. The books fell out in an instant, but their trajectory resonated in my mind like a slow-motion wail of defeat. I knew at that moment that we had crossed a line. I could no longer muster up the will to chase after Taro and his assignments. I had no energy left for those battles. The idea of any more confrontation in the confines of our apartment was suddenly repulsive. I was done.

In the previous year, I had already set some wheels into motion for us to relocate to the US. I had researched and even applied to some schools for Taro there, but my feelings then were half-hearted. These were distant backup plans made while I fantasized that Taro would suddenly shape up and fit in at The School and The Junior High. I initially had looked for public schools in New York City. I chose New York because my brother and his family lived there. Having a family member in a new city would be an immense source of support, and Taro loved his cousins. But the reputable public schools had large classes and were in expensive neighborhoods. I then emailed the admission offices of several private schools. They all replied that they would not take a seventh grader who didn't speak English. Meanwhile several friends urged me to consider boarding school. The idea of sending Taro away at age twelve was horrifying. I understood my friends' arguments intellectually; that boarding schools knew how to teach all sorts of kids, Taro would mature by living away from home, and the schools offered great English language instruction for foreign students. The significance of mastering English was a no-brainer. It has changed my life in that, among other things, I always have job opportunities teaching and translating in Japan where relatively few people speak English well. But the other good reasons to send Taro away fell on my deaf ears. That is, until those cascading books woke me into action.

"You're going to boarding school," I announced to Taro soon after the locker epiphany.

"No. No way," came the reply. We "discussed" it off and on. On a good day, I told him how exciting the new challenge would be. On a bad day I said, "I told you I'd send you to boarding school if you didn't do your homework."

Three months into the seventh grade, Taro stood in front of his homeroom class and sheepishly said he would be leaving. One boy tried to cheer up the stunned and despondent students by declaring, "I'll take over as the mood-maker of the class."

A few girls huddled in the stairwell at recess and cried. The school's *kendo* or Japanese fencing team Taro had joined arranged a special send-off where he ran a gauntlet of honor, passing between two rows of upperclassmen while crossing bamboo swords with them along the way. The day of his announcement I crafted personalized emails about our move to every mother I knew, carefully sending them out one after another so they would be received at around the same time. I didn't write that we were fleeing our failures but that we were moving because I was relocating to the US for work. On Taro's last day at school, his classmates threw him up in the air and caught him on the way down; a traditional Japanese practice where someone who has achieved a great milestone gets a celebratory toss. That night I stood by his bed and stared at him sprawled out in deep slumber in the room where we had clashed nearly every day. Soon he would leave this nest and probably never live with me again except for holidays. How could I have let this happen? As I stood there staring at him, I wanted to scream and tear up the room and run out of the apartment. I wanted to wake up and find Taro small again. To do it over.

During our first week in the US, Taro kept his watch on Japan time, periodically pointing out what his classmates must be up to.

"Maechin is waking up now," he would say in the evening on the East Coast about a classmate back in Tokyo where the sun was rising. When we were unpacking in his dormitory room, he found a one-yen coin in his bag and pressed it against his cheek.

"It's so nice and cool," he said, closing his eyes to savor the sensation. "It reminds me of Japan."

But within a few weeks there were no more signs of sentimental nostalgia. Taro was casually jostling with his new classmates from all over the world, playing computer games on his laptop while sitting on his dorm bed, throwing a Frisbee around, and blowing off steam in the gym. What a privileged world he had entered. The boarding school was located on eight-hundred acres of verdant, hilly grounds in western Massachusetts that included a pond stocked with trout for fishing, stand-alone dormitories, and classroom buildings and, most stunning to us, its own ski slope, complete with chairlift and ski jump. When I first saw the school, I had been with my brother and turned to say to him, "Isn't this the most beautiful school you've ever seen?" He replied that the boarding school his sons attended was "more beautiful," which taught me the lavish standards of wealthy private schools in the United States.

Our new life turned out to be a more difficult adjustment for me than for Taro. I had come over with two suitcases, not intending to stay for long. But when I found out there would be events at school or holidays for Taro nearly every month, I decided I wanted to stay in the same time zone, close enough for frequent visits, and rented an apartment in New York City. I made inquiries about jobs that were looking for bilingual employees but soon concluded that working full-time would defeat the purpose of my relocation. So I continued my free-lance writing and translating and relied heavily on my savings and financial help from my father. Life in the US was not com-pletely foreign to me. I had gone to junior high school and high school in Washington, D.C., while my father worked there, and later I had spent two years in graduate school in Hono-lulu. But this was the first time I was living abroad on my own. I had no network of friends in New York City, and the usual stress of getting used to living in a new place was compounded by the hole in my life left by the absence of Taro. My musings in the *New York Times* at the time reflect my disorientation. The first column I wrote after our move, titled "Acclimating from Tokyo to New York City,"[28] had me deep in sentimental self-pity, rubbing a charm with Taro's name engraved on it and telling myself to be the steady arc described in a poem by Khalil Gibran: "*You are the bows from which your children as living*

---

28 http://www.nytimes.com/2011/08/11/opinion/11iht-edmakihara11.html

arrows are sent forth."[29] I followed up a few months later with "The Comfort of Courtesy,"[30] which grumbled about lax standards of service in the US compared to my beloved Japan. And two months later I even chronicled my fear of dropping dead in my apartment with no one noticing my demise, in "Afraid of Dying Alone."[31]

I didn't elicit much sympathy. I wasn't exactly living hand-to-mouth, after all, with an apartment in Manhattan and a son in boarding school. A few days after the death column ran, the *New York Times* printed a letter from a reader in France who wrote, "If Ms. Makihara would stop focusing on the negatives and start appreciating the positives (the great mix of diverse people, the rich cultural life, etc.) she would be a lot happier."[32] Another friend, in an email, reminded me of the word for perseverance in Japanese, saying, "There might be some need for more *gaman*." In a handwritten, three-page letter, my father urged me to take the opportunity of Taro away at school to achieve something. "I feel this might be the last opportunity for you to realize your inherent talent," he wrote, offering to finance such endeavors. "Time is of the essence. We hope to enjoy longevity, but as you know anything can happen."

My parents mailed me Japanese books with titles like, *Global Career: There is a Path Open for Great Possibilities for*

29 Khalil Gibran, *The Prophet* (New York: Alfred A. Knopf, 1923), 17.

30 http://www.nytimes.com/2011/10/08/opinion/08iht-edmakihara08
.html

31 http://www.nytimes.com/2012/04/10/opinion/afraid-of-dying-
alone.html

32 http://www.nytimes.com/2011/10/12/opinion/12iht-edlet12.html

Everyone[33] or *Fly Out from Your Tiny "Birdcage,"*[34] both written by high-profile Japanese women with impeccable academic and business credentials who championed global thinking. Although I never followed my father's career suggestions, I also felt I was in no position to counter anything he said. I was the age my father was when he ran the entire operations in North and South America for Japan's largest trading company.

While I shrugged off his urgings to expand my work, I did note one of my father's musings buried deep toward the end of the letter. "I think you should be preparing and investing now for the goal of being not a source of dependency for Taro, but someone he respects." I sometimes worried how Taro would recall our battles. Would I be forever remembered as the "ogre" he once described me as in a diary? I'd never thought about a concept as big as "respect." Did I respect my parents? It's hard not to admire my father's success as an executive and his wide network of friends around the world. I could look up to my mother's intellect, charm, and wit that allowed her to hold her own alongside my father despite not finishing college or developing a profession. As for their parenting, however, I am bitter that, while well-intentioned, they labeled my brother as the smart one and encouraged him toward academic and professional achievements, but viewed me as a girl who should seek happiness in marriage with a job on the side. A friend once told me, "It's interesting how when your father talks about your brother he's talking about an adult. But when he talks about you, it sounds like he's talking about a three-year-old."

---

33 Written by Yoko Ishikura, published in 2011 by Toyo Keizai Shinpo, Tokyo.

34 Written by Eriko Kawai, published in 2013 by Diamond, Tokyo.

I hoped I would not be describing Taro that way when he was an adult. But I may be headed in that direction. So far, I had made all decisions, large and small, for Taro. I treated him like a small extension of myself. I didn't want to be urging Taro to switch careers when he was in his fifties.

•

I chose the boarding school partly because of some similarities it shared with The School. Both were private institutions with histories dating back to the early 1900s. They had close-knit alumni groups that were proud of their alma maters and its traditions. Both schools were located amid beautiful greenery. Their academic and athletic standards were high. But the differences were far more prevalent.

First of all, everything was so much more informal in the US. Before one parents' meeting, Taro's English teacher sent me an email inviting me to a girls' night out with another teacher to "put our feet up and our hair down." In Japan, the teacher is the master and never a friend. When parents were observing a science class at the boarding school, a teacher asked the students, "What is surface tension?" One mother blurted out jokingly, "When you're fighting with your husband?" American parents sometimes raised their hands to ask questions during class or even answered those meant for students. At The School, we always stood stiffly and silently in the back and hoped that our children would do well enough not to embarrass us. The parents and children at the boarding school came from diverse backgrounds—from around the country and the world, with only about 20 percent from the local area. About a fourth of the students were on some sort of financial aid. So there was no culture of reining in mothers who stood out. In fact, unless you lived close to the school, it was difficult to interact much with the other parents since you only saw them on parent visitation days a few times a year.

I also found a much more casual attitude toward learning and developmental disorders as well as the usage of medication for them. Almost every parent at the boarding school I met had a child with some sort of learning issue or knew someone who struggled. In my six years at The School, the subject of ADHD came up only once in my conversations with parents. One mother was describing how she had taken her son to a doctor because he was so reluctant to study.

"But they said there was nothing wrong with him, no ADHD or anything," she said, expressing her great relief and suggesting that ADHD would have been a worst-case scenario.

Taro's Japanese psychiatrist and I had agreed to put Taro on medication as a last resort and only temporarily to help him get through the most rigid years of schooling. At the boarding school, every new fall term I tried to start Taro off without the drugs in the hopes he would learn to cope without them. But all his teachers urged me to begin the year with Taro on the medication. They reasoned that otherwise he might falter at the beginning and damage his self-esteem. He can go off them later if he is doing well, they said. I stubbornly started Taro without the medication anyway, only to have him struggle right away so that I reluctantly put him back on them. They seemed to help slightly in keeping him focused for longer periods of time. After a few years, Taro decided he no longer wanted the hassle of collecting his medication from the school nurse each morning. He may have performed better in school on the drugs, but he didn't fail or seem unhappy without them, so I suppose he had found his coping methods alongside some advancements that came with maturity.

The most striking contrast between the two school systems was the amount of positive reinforcement doled out in the US. His first report card comments from the boarding school praised his progress and happiness without referring to any of his grades. The teacher wrote, "Taro is showing improvement and greater understanding in his classes. He seems to enjoy what he is doing, and he has a positive attitude." Could this be the same boy beaten for insolence in Japan? In the US, there was a constant attempt to look at things from the bright side. An incorrect response to a teacher's question was often met by "Oh, that comes later," rather than an outright "No." Criticism came couched in what seemed like a desperate attempt to keep the tone upbeat by avoiding the negative form, like in the wording of the following evaluation on Taro's art work: "*Neatness, attention to detail, accurate glass-cutting skills, productive use of class time, all came with some resistance.*" Many parents, too, related to their children this way. I overheard one mother say to a teacher about her son, "Oh, we love him. He has absolutely no issues." That had my Japanese modesty wiring cringing. If you wanted to play sports but were not a super athlete, no problem. In addition to varsity, there were one or two more teams for less rigorous players. At The Junior High, there was usually just one team per sport so that some students warmed the bench the entire three years of middle school. In case anything was overlooked amid this supportive boarding school environment, the American teachers urged the students to become "self-advocates." They must learn to ask for help when they need it, speaking up for themselves. This would be a huge challenge for Taro, coming from the Japanese classroom where attracting attention to oneself was never a virtue.

And then, there was the food. "You got so fat!" were the first words out of my mouth when I saw Taro step out of the bus on his first visit home after two months at boarding school. His oval face had puffed into chubby cheeks. It must have been the shift in diet from fresh fish, vegetables, tofu, and rice in Japan, to the all-you-can eat American diet of meat, bread, and salad bar (which he avoided).

•

Taro's most obvious achievement at his new school was his mastery of the English language. He simply absorbed it by living twenty-four seven in an English-speaking environment. Taro became fluent after one year and a native speaker in two. I watched, thrilled, as he began to pronounce popular teen words like "awkward" and "awesome" with deliberate exaggeration on the first syllable and appeared entranced by his own new sounds. It reminded me of my own language awakening when I was his age and moved from Tokyo to Seattle. I remember the morning on the school bus when I struggled to convey the word "patrol" to the girl sitting next to me as I tried to ask her about the sixth-grade traffic duties. I endured many humiliating moments like that when I had to repeat the same word over and over to what seemed like my tone-deaf classmates. Then one day I lay awake in bed and suddenly found my thoughts streaming out in English words, like a magic spell had taken over my tongue. Taro must have had that moment, too. At first when I phoned him at school to see how he was doing, he replied in clipped Japanese phrases like, "*bestu ni,*" or "not much." After a few months, he came back to me in English: "Just chillin'."

Another clear advantage to the move was that we were no longer at loggerheads every day. But soon I began to look back at some of the green grass we had left behind. Was Taro stocking up enough on the fundamental knowledge needed for critical thinking further down the line? In seventh grade at the US school, Taro had four or five academic subjects such as English, math and science, and several non-academic subjects like art or chess. In Japan, he had struggled with that heavy load of fourteen classes. At the US school the non-academic classes were decidedly relaxed and often graded on a pass/fail basis. In the Japanese school, all of the subjects were graded with homework and project requirements. Taro's American teachers patiently tailored his instruction to his level instead of leaving it up to him (and me) to try to catch up to the class average as we were expected to in Japan. In fact, the US school's motto was "to meet boys where they are." It sounds great, but I wondered, does that mean a boy might stay at that level? The US teachers patiently tried to guide Taro into independent, analytical thinking. But shouldn't they also be pushing him to memorize as many facts as possible to build up the foundation from where such thoughts would arise? Was I still a believer in the Japanese educational model that failed us? Was there a happy medium somewhere? Anywhere? In the years after putting Taro in a US school, I would question its teaching methods and materials. But one thing I never wavered on was my decision to leave Japan. We had been misfits there and hurled our outcast frustrations against each other. Now at least, it seemed we faced a common challenge: the beast of learning that Taro would face alone at boarding school with the support I would throw to him from a distance.

For his part, Taro appeared to be relishing this newfound emancipation. "Free time in the US really means free," he told me when I asked him shortly after our move what he found different between the US and Japanese schools. "In Japan, free time means you're free to do everything you're not free to do."

January 19, 2010

I am always near last, but today I ran really hard and came in 5th. I think it's because today we ran 2 kilometers for the first time. It was strange that I was running in the lead pack without really knowing what I was doing. At first, I was chasing after them like goldfish droppings. And at the end of the first lap, Hayashi-kun told me I was in 6th place at 4 minutes 14 seconds. I remember that much. One kilometer is easy, so I was sprinting from the start. I have lots of experience with 2 kilometers. You run with big strides like you are jumping. That's how I made it to the goal. After I ran into the goal, I fell down and crossed my arms like a pharaoh. I put my cap over my face and dreamed of becoming MVP.

Looking Back

June 6, 2017

• • •

Up ahead on the highway looms a double-arched gateway with KOKSHETAU written in big blue letters across the top.

"Where are the blue triangles?" I ask our driver, showing him the photo of the town sign in the "adoption book" I had put together for Taro eighteen years ago, filled with pictures from that time.

"Oh, that's old. It's gone," he says.

Taro rotates the photo around to orient himself to find the cemetery. It's still there, to the left, with the town to the right. As we drive into the city center I see none of the abandoned buildings etched into my memory of a dying town. Today the city feels normal. There are tree-lined boulevards, an amusement park and a shopping mall where I stop to buy some fridge magnets that say Kokshetau on them. I show Taro a black-and-white-knitted hat and scarf that bear the city name.

"I'd never wear that style," he says, and goes back to searching for a Wi-Fi signal on his phone. People come up and ask Taro for directions; he looks like any other Kazakh young man. He smiles a little and shakes his head and waves his hand to signal, apologetically, that he doesn't speak Russian or Kazakh. I buy the hat and scarf for myself. I'm so excited to be with Taro on this journey back to his roots.

"That was a hard, hard time," Dr. Natalia says, sipping a cappuccino in a café where an odd assortment of suitcases, skis, and an umbrella line a shelf along the ceiling for decor. Taro's first pediatrician is blond now, retired from the Kokshetau maternity hospital and running another medical facility. We were remembering 1999, the year that Taro was born, back when every month several babies were left abandoned at the hospital. Now there are no foreign adoptions, and a long line of Kazakhs are waiting to adopt the few babies that need homes, Natalia says. She recalls, laughing, how during those bleak years a group of foreigners visiting the hospital were shocked to see crates of vodka stacked up in a doctor's office.

"They thought we really must drink a lot, but we were actually just getting paid in vodka because the employer had no money to give out," she said.

Natalia also has an eighteen-year-old son. We exchange pleasantries about how our boys only communicate with us when they want something. I quickly bring Natalia up to date, that I divorced and moved back to Japan and raised Taro there until I brought us to the US when he was twelve. And now he's getting ready to go off to college.

"Wonderful," she says, looking over to him sitting beside her. She nods and smiles as if the time and distance from then to now were one smooth and happy memory.

•

How should I assess the years since Natalia lifted that help-less creature out of the crib and handed him over to me eighteen years ago? I think about the tunnel vision I had trying to make Taro perform each task at hand for the sake of doing that task well—or at least as well as his classmates. But did he take away valuable lessons from The School?

Taro is still disorganized and distracted, traits that keep him a B student, but he knows Japanese history, can do math in his head, and still loves to read. He's still an ace at socializing and accumulating friends. Good. The group mentality at The School instilled in him the ability to take one for the team. And he's maintained his innate kindness, sense of humor, and a bit of shyness, all of which make him approachable and well-liked. Taro's high school teachers say he is polite and respectful which I attribute in part to The School's culture of deference to elders. Self-esteem? I worry deeply. The constant poor assessments and scoldings at The School, climaxing in the beating, had to have damaged his sense of worth. And at home, I had yelled at Taro nearly every day and rushed him constantly and pushed him to study late into the night.

And yet, considering all of that, Taro today appears remark-ably unscathed. He says he loved his boarding schools, was on the soccer and ski teams, and has always had close friends. But he's quick to say, "I don't test well," and even, "I'm not smart." So, it was all the more meaningful when Taro was recruited by several colleges to play soccer, some even offering gener-ous scholarships. The coaches called and texted him, telling him what a special addition he would make to their teams. I realized it was probably the first time in his life that Taro felt truly wanted. His birth mother had abandoned him, his father stopped contacting us, and I was never satisfied.

I don't know what makes Taro who he is today apart from a vague notion that he must be an amalgam of everything including what he was born with. And what am I to him? His diary entries show that I was an unwavering part of his universe, both as an enjoyable playmate and unreasonable brute.

While we were traveling on a high-speed train through the Japanese countryside recently, I asked Taro, "What do you remember about those days when you went to The School?"

"You were always telling me to hurry up. You were so impatient. You always made cold breakfasts," he said.

I had to laugh. "You know what, Taro?" I said. "That's exactly how you would describe me now. It's like nothing's changed."

"That's right," he replied, and began laughing, too, just as our train emerged from a tunnel and raced past another town.

March 9, 2010

To Diary in Appreciation of Diary
   I am turning 11 years old for the first time in my life.
   I'm sorry I dropped you and lost you. You always took it quietly, and I feel sorry for you.

Acknowledgments

· · ·

THIS BOOK IS AN EXPRESSION OF LOVE, REMORSE, AND gratitude. Thank you, Taro, for the immeasurable joy you brought into my life with your free spirit that would not be crushed. Your endearing humor and boundless resilience inspired me to write this book.

I am indebted to Skyhorse publisher Tony Lyons who took a chance on a first-time author and to Alejandro Carosso and Hector Carosso, who introduced me to Tony. Lisa Kaufman patiently walked me through the process of taking a manuscript to publication. Lilly Golden's deft editing lifted my writing. Wendy Vissar found the perfect light for my photos and the right tone for my website.

Many friends supported me throughout this process. They are too many to name here, but I would like to mention those who read the manuscript and offered wise feedback: Susan Essoyan, Mary Macvean, Nancy Matsumoto, Jean Roth, and Marilyn Wyatt.

I started writing this book at the New York Public Library where Jay Barcsdale placed me in the Wertheim Room. I was able to continue writing at Columbia University due to the generosity of the Weatherhead East Asian Institute and the support of Professors Carol Gluck, Hugh Patrick, and Gerald Curtis. I first began writing about my family for the *New York Times Magazine* and the then *International Herald Tribune* under the encouragement and guidance of Serge Schmemann and Brian Zittel.

Finally, I owe everything to my family, Ben and Kiko Makihara, Jun Makihara and Mimi Oka, and of course, Taro.